Landscapes of
MADEIRA

a countryside guide
Eighth edition

John and Pat Underwood

SUNFLOWER BOOKS

Eighth edition © 2005
Sunflower Books™
PO Box 36160
London SW7 3WS, UK
www.sunflowerbooks.co.uk

Published in the USA by
Hunter Publishing Inc
130 Campus Drive
Edison, NJ 08818
www.hunterpublishing.com

ISBN 1-85691-264-7

Levada do Furado (Walk 25)

Important note to the reader

We have tried to ensure that the descriptions and maps in this book
are error-free at press date. *Be sure to check our web site for an 'Update' before you travel* (see inside front cover). It is very helpful for
us to receive your comments (sent in care of the publishers, please)
for the updating of future printings.

   We rely on those who use this book — especially walkers — to
take along a good supply of common sense when they explore. Conditions change very rapidly on Madeira, and *storm damage or bulldozing may make a route unsafe at any time.* If the route is not as
we outline it here, and your way ahead is not secure, return to the
point of departure. *Never attempt to complete a tour or walk under hazardous conditions!* Please read carefully the notes on pages
35 to 40, the Country code on page 8, and the introductory comments at the beginning of each tour and walk (regarding road conditions, equipment, grade, distances and time, etc). Explore *safely*,
while at the same time respecting the beauty of the countryside.

*Cover photograph: old trail below the Cabeço da Vigia, seen from
   São Jorge (Walk 18)*
Title page: the high peaks from the ER104 near Rosário

Photographs: John Underwood
Maps: John Underwood, adapted from Portuguese IGC/military
   maps; see 'Acknowledgements', page 7
A CIP catalogue record for this book is available from the British
   Library.
Printed and bound in England: J H Haynes & Co Ltd

10 9 8 7 6 5 4 3 2 1

Contents

4　Landscapes of Madeira

Pico Grande from the flanks of Pico do Arieiro

Preface

Since we first published a small book of Madeira walks in 1980, not only has *Landscapes of Madeira* become the most widely used walkers' guide on the island, but it inspired a whole series of *Landscapes* books, which we publish under our Sunflower imprint. The aim of the series is to lead the visitor off the beaten track and into the countryside — whether by car, public transport, or on foot.

Many changes have come about since the last edition of this book was published just over two years ago — mostly as the result of intensive road-building. But this is *not* all bad news for walkers. No walks have been badly affected, and the new roads are proving to be a boon: motorists can now get to almost any walk on the island in an hour, and faster roads have enabled many of the bus companies to extend their existing services (eg bus 156) or add new routes (eg bus 56). The plan is to create a *Via Rápida* encircling the island, as well as a fast link up the centre (between Ribeira Brava and São Vicente). Naturally there have again been major changes to the maps, and we do think that these are the most accurate maps available.

All Sunflower authors hope to convey more than mere enthusiasm for their chosen landscapes — love might be a better word. Our love affair with Madeira really came into blossom with our 'discovery' of the levadas. They never cease to fascinate or inspire us. No matter how tired we may be, to walk beside a levada always refreshes our spirits and brings the bounce back into our steps.

The levadas

Whether you use this book to tour, walk or picnic, we will lead you along the levadas. Such watercourses are not unique to Madeira: what *is* unique is their **accessibility** and **extent**. You need only venture a little way off the main roads to begin to appreciate Madeira's myriad aqueducts — for their beauty, ingenuity of design, and for the courage and determination needed to bring the concept to its present glory. The island's irrigation system now comprises about 2500km (1550 miles) of channels, including 50km (30 miles) of tunnels — and the work started centuries ago.

The earliest settlers on Madeira began cultivating the lower slopes in the south of the island, cutting out small terraces *(poios)* like those shown on page 7. Working with contractors (who sometimes used slave or convict labour),

Tiny streams feed the Levada da Negra (Walk 2).

they built the first small levadas, which carried water from springs higher up the mountainsides to irrigate their lands. These narrow watercourses (see left) plummet downhill, rushing and frothing with energy; their banks are often festooned with wild flowers.

By the early 1900s, there were about 200 of these levadas, meandering over about 1000km (620 miles). Many were privately owned, and the undisciplined appropriation of water meant that the island's most valuable asset was often unfairly distributed. In fact, by the mid 1930s, only two-thirds of the island's arable land was under cultivation — and just half of that was irrigated. Only the State had the money to implement a major building programme and the authority to enforce a more equitable system of distribution.

For there was plenty of water for irrigation, and torrents to spare for power. Clouds driven to the island by the prevailing northerly winds are caught by the central mountain chain, and as much as 2m (80 inches) of rain may fall in the north in a year, while the south coast may be almost dry for up to six months. In effect the island is a huge self-regulating reservoir. Rain seeps down into the porous volcanic ash but, on meeting impervious layers of rock, it wells up again in springs. Unless this rainwater is channelled, it just runs down ravines and into the sea.

In 1939 the Portuguese government sent a mission to the island to study an irrigation/hydroelectric scheme. The 'new' levadas created from its plans — wide mini-canals — contour through the valleys; their flow is stately and serene, and their banks are lovingly planted with agapanthus lilies and hydrangeas. These wide waterways are first channelled out at an altitude of about 1000m/3300ft, where the concentration of rainfall, dew and springs is greatest. The water is then piped down to the power stations lying just at the outer edge of the arable land (about 600m/2000ft), from where it flows on to the irrigated zones. Here, distribution is carried out by the *levadeiro*, who diverts the flow to each proprietor.

Terraces (poios) *in the Ribeira dos Socorridos (Walk 1)*

Although work is on-going, most of the mission's development plans were implemented by 1970. Among the most important projects were the Levada do Norte and the Levada dos Tornos, both of which you will discover as you tour, walk or picnic. Their incredible length, considering the terrain, is best gauged on the fold-out touring map. The work took only 25 years to complete, although it was all done by hand. How were the tunnels cut through the solid basalt? How did the workers channel out the levadas beneath the icy waterfalls, halfway between earth and sky? Often, as during the construction of the old corniche road ('Antiga 101'; see Car tour 5) between São Vicente and Porto Moniz, they were suspended from above in wicker baskets, while they fought the unyielding stone with picks. Many lost their lives to bring water and electricity to the islanders … and unending joy to walkers.

Acknowledgements

We are very grateful for the invaluable help of everyone who contacts us with update suggestions. For this Eighth edition, we wish to thank Sr Felipe Ferreira of the Departamento de Obras in Funchal, for helping us unravel the ongoing saga of Madeira's roads and, of course, the Instituto Geográfico e Cadastral, for permission to adapt their maps.

Most of all, this book is dedicated to the memory of those who set us on our way and helped enormously with the first few editions: John and Richard Blandy, José Fernandes, Jim Leahy and Luís de Sousa.

Recommended reading

There are now several good general guides available; any written by Christopher Catling will be up-to-date.

Levadas and footpaths of Madeira by Raimundo Quintal (available on Madeira) will be of interest to all keen walkers who want to know more about the island's flora and ecology. We do not recommend it as a *guide,* but it contains a wealth of background information for which there is no space in our book.

Madeira walk and eat (Sunflower 2005) is our new guide. Ten of the walks are in this book, and there are three new routes. The walk descriptions are complemented by information about restaurants and cafés en route, with their menus — and recipes for you to cook at home.

Country code for walkers and motorists

The experienced rambler is used to following a 'country code', but the tourist out for a lark may unwittingly cause damage, harm animals, and even endanger his own life. Please respect this country code.

- **Only light fires at purpose-built fireplaces.**
- **Do not damage levadas.** Don't touch sluice gates or the stones used to control small sluices.
- **Protect all wild and cultivated plants.** Picking flowers or uprooting plants *is now illegal.* Never cross cultivated land!
- **Take all your litter away with you.**
- **Do not frighten animals.** They are not tame. By making loud noises, or trying to touch or photograph them, you may cause them to run in fear — over a precipice.
- **Leave all gates as you find them.** They have a purpose: generally to keep animals in — or out of — an area.
- **Walkers — DO NOT TAKE RISKS!** And remember:
- **At any time a walk may become unsafe.** If the route is not as we describe it, if mists are falling, or if it is late in the day, *turn back!* Remember, there is *virtually no twilight on Madeira!*
- **NEVER walk alone** — and **always** tell a responsible person *exactly* where you are going and what time you plan to return.
- **Do not overestimate your capacity:** your speed will be determined by the slowest walker in the group, and bus connections may be vital.
- **Proper footwear is essential.** Flat clay paths can be deceptive; when they are damp they can be as slippery as ice.
- **Mists can fall suddenly** on the Paúl da Serra and in the mountains.
- **Warm clothing** and **extra rations** are needed in the mountains.
- **Compass, whistle, torch, first-aid kit and mobile phone** weigh little, but might save your life. In case of emergency, use your mobile to call 112 (the emergency number throughout the EU).
- **Protect yourself from the sun.**
- **A stout stick** is a help on steep terrain and to discourage the rare unfriendly dog (see also note on page 38, 'Nuisances').
- **Read and re-read the 'Important note'** on page 2 and guidelines on grade and equipment for each walk you plan to do.

Ancient laurels in the Fanal (Car tour 5)

❀ Getting about

There is no doubt that a **hired car** or taxi is the most convenient way of getting round the island. We hope that the liberal cross-references to picnics and walks in the touring section will inspire motorists and walkers to team up on car hire. The walking maps show the car symbol (🚗) only at the *parking* places we recommend in the text; if friends can drop you off or collect you, look on the maps for places where roads cross the walks.

All **taxi** drivers carry a government-approved price list for journeys outside Funchal. Your hotel porter can suggest a driver for an all-day tour: many are knowledgeable about island culture and customs; some are even keen walkers!

Coach tours are the most popular way of 'seeing Madeira in a day'. They provide a painless introduction to road conditions and a remarkable overview of island scenery.

Since most of the best walks on Madeira are linear (see page 35), you will come to appreciate the **local interurban bus** network. The system is economical, reliable and safe. The town plan on the following pages shows you where to board your bus in Funchal; all buses depart from the Avenida do Mar. At time of writing, there are three main operators: Rodoeste (www.rodoeste.pt), SAM (no web site) and Horarios do Funchal. (www.horariosdofunchal.pt). Tickets are bought at their kiosks near the departure points, or on the bus.

Please do not rely *solely* on our **bus timetables** (pages 138-142); changes are fairly frequent. For minimal cost you can buy a booklet of timetables ('Madeira by Bus') at the nearest tourist office,* or update our timetables at the various operators' bus stations or kiosks in Funchal. *Do arrive early for your bus!* It may take you several minutes to find the one you want, and they leave spot on time!

Orange town buses (as well as some interurban routes) are operated by Horarios do Funchal. *Do* call at their office in Anadia Shopping (11-1pm Mon-Sat, also 5-9pm Mon-Fri) and collect their little booklets 'Transportes Urbanos' and 'Transportes Interurbanos' — as well as city bus fare-saving tickets (see notes at the top of page 142). These little booklets, with route maps, are invaluable. (By the way, do not confuse identical bus numbers: orange town bus 29 to Romeiros; white/yellow/silver interurban bus 29 to Camacha!)

*This booklet is very useful, as it also shows the bus liveries and routes. Note, too, that local tourist offices (eg Santana, Ribeira Brava) usually have free handouts which may list *additional* buses serving their areas.

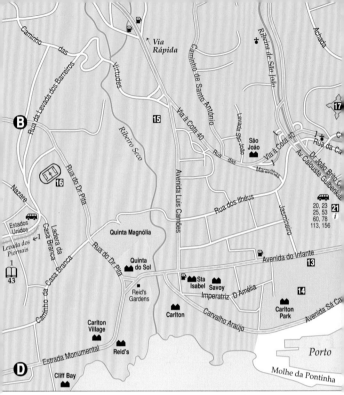

1	Tourist Offices	
2	Infante Fountains	
3	Madeira Balloon	
4	Air Portugal (TAP)	
5	Municipal Theatre	
6	Casa do Turista	
7	Government Offices	
8	Sé (Cathedral)	
9	Parliament (Old Customs House)	
10	Monte toboggan terminus	
11	Anadia Shopping, Horarios Office	
12	Santa Caterina Chapel	
13	Quinta Vigia (President's House)	
14	Casino	
15	Hospital	
16	Barreiros Stadium	
17	Forte do Pico	
18	Quinta das Cruzes	
19	Santa Clara Convent	

20	Municipal Museum
21	Post Office, SAM Bus Station
22	São Lourenço Palace
23	Collegiate Church
24	Madeira Wine Institute
25	Law Courts
26	Town Hall
27	Museum of Sacred Art
28	New Customs House
29	Market
30	Forte de São Tiago
31	Old Town
32	Boat Trips
33	Museum of Electricity
34	Embroidery Museum
35	Rodoeste Bus Station
36	EACL and Horarios Interurban Buses
37	Cable Car to Babosas and Car Park
38	Sugar Museum, Rodoeste (N° 50-52)

BUS DEPARTURES (*i*: bus information kiosk, ticket sales)

N°	Destination	from	Company (and Livery)
2	Assomada	**36**	EACL (grey/red)
3	Estreito de Câmara de Lobos	**9**	Rodoeste (cream/red)*
4	Madalena do Mar	**9**	Rodoeste (cream/red)*
6	Arco de São Jorge via ER104	**9**	Rodoeste (cream/red)*
7	Ribeira Brava	**9**	Rodoeste (cream/red)*
20	Santo da Serra	opposite **9**	SAM (cream/green)
23	Machico	opposite **9**	SAM (cream/green)

*buses to tourist destinations are *white*

10

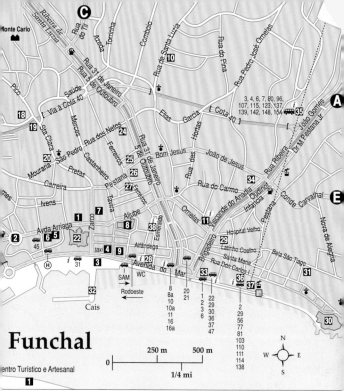

Funchal

	250 m	500 m
0		
	1/4 mi	

N ↑ / S ↓, W ← → E

Centro Turístico e Artesanal **1**

N°	Destination	from	Company (and Livery)
29	Camacha	**36**	Horarios (white/yellow/silver)
53	Faial	*opposite* **9**	SAM (cream/green)
56	Santana via Faial	**36**	Horarios (white/yellow/silver)
60	Boqueirão	*opposite* **9**	SAM (cream/green)
77	Santo da Serra	**36**	Horarios (white/yellow/silver)
78	Machico, Faial	*opposite* **9**	SAM (cream/green)
80	Porto Moniz	**9**	Rodoeste (cream/red)*
81	Curral das Freiras	**36**	Horarios (white/yellow/silver)
96	Corticeiras	**9**	Rodoeste (cream/red)*
103	Arco de São Jorge via ER103	**36**	Horarios (white/yellow/silver)
110	Boqueirão via Caniço	**36**	Horarios (white/yellow/silver)
111	Achadinha	**36**	Horarios (white/yellow/silver)
113	Machico, Caniçal	*opposite* **9**	SAM (cream/green)
114	Nogueira	**36**	Horarios (white/yellow/silver)
115	Estreito da Calheta	**9**	Rodoeste (cream/red)*
123	Campanário	**9**	Rodoeste (cream/red)*
138	São Jorge (Cabanas)	**36**	Horarios (white/yellow/silver)
139	Porto Moniz	**9**	Rodoeste (cream/red)*
142	Ponta do Pargo	**9**	Rodoeste (cream/red)*
148	Boa Morte	**9**	Rodoeste (cream/red)*
154	Cabo Girão	**9**	Rodoeste (cream/red)*
156	Machico, Maroços	*opposite* **9**	SAM (cream/green)

ORANGE TOWN BUSES (Horarios do Funchal)

1, 3	Lombada		29	Romeiros	*east of* **33**
2	Quebradas	**33**	30	Jardim Botânico	*east of* **33**
8, 16	Santa Quitéria	*east of* **28**	31	Jardim Botânico	*opposite* **22**
11	Trapiche	*east of* **28**	36, 37	Palheiro Ferreiro	*east of* **33**
20, 21	Monte	*northeast of* **28**	45	Stadium	*opposite* **6**
22	Babosas	*east of* **33**	47	São João Latrão	*east of* **33**

11

Picnicking

In the course of some of our rambles we've come upon easy-to-reach picnic spots that might appeal to those of you who prefer *very* short walks. If you are car touring, they are an 'off-the-beaten-track' alternative to the island's many roadside picnic tables.

All the information you need to find these more secluded picnic spots is given below, where *picnic numbers correspond to walk numbers,* so that you can quickly find the general location on the island by looking at the touring map. We give you walking times and transport details. The location of the picnic is indicated by the green-printed symbol *P* on the appropriate *walking map,* which also shows the nearest 🚍 stop (if appropriate) and 🚗 parking area. Most of the picnic settings are illustrated.

Please remember to **wear sensible shoes and take a sunhat** (the symbol ○ after the title indicates a picnic **in full sun**). It's a good idea to take along a plastic groundsheet as well, in case it's damp or prickly.

If you are travelling by bus, check the latest schedules (see page 9). **Travelling by car**, park *well off* the road; *never* block a road or track. **All picnickers should read the Country code on page 8 and go quietly in the countryside.**

2 POÇO DA NEVE, ARIEIRO (map on reverse of touring map, photograph opposite) ○

🚗 ice house (Poço da Neve); it lies *below* the road, hidden by a stone wall edging a small parking bay, 2km below Pico do Arieiro (Car tours 1, 4). **Up to 5min on foot.** *Picnic by the ice house (no shade), or below it in the heath tree grove.* **Splendid view over moors, down to Funchal.**

3 EIRA DO SERRADO (map on reverse of touring map, photograph pages 46-47)

🚗 (Car tour 3) to the Eira do Serrado. **5min on foot.** Or 🚍 81 to the Eira turn-off on the ER107. **20min on foot.** *Follow Walk 3 (pages 47-48) from the 15min-point for five minutes.* **Fine view over Curral, away from the crowds.**

6 BOA MORTE (map pages 54-55, photograph page 56)

🚗 or 🚍 127 to Boa Morte. By car, turn north off the ER229 3km west of Campanário (signposted: 'S João, S Paulo, Levada do Norte'; Car tour 6). Continue past Boa Morte to the Levada do Norte (3.5km from the ER229), where you can park. **Up to 35min on foot.** By bus follow Short walk 6-3, page 55, returning on 🚍 148. **Up to 45min on foot.** *Turn left (northwest) on the levada.* **The forest itself is an exceptionally lovely setting, or continue on the levada for magnificent views of the Ribeira Brava and the Paúl da Serra. Good shade.**

The Santa Luzia Valley and Funchal from the Poço da Neve ('snow pit' or 'ice house'). Walk and Picnic 2; Car tours 1 and 4

7a PORTO NOVO FROM THE EAST (map pages 62-63)

🚗 or 🚌 60 (Boqueirão bus) to the Levada dos Tornos. **15-20min on foot.** By car, take the ER206 south from Águas Mansas (Car tour 2) and park by the levada, 1.6km downhill. By bus, ask the driver for 'Levada dos Tornos, Lombo Grande'; the levada is a minute uphill from the stop. *Head west on the levada: 10 minutes' walking will give you good views, or go as far as the tunnel with 'windows' mentioned on page 64 (20min).* **This picnic overlooks the western side of the Porto Novo Valley and is at its best in spring. Some shade nearby.**

7b BOAVENTURA VALLEY (map pages 62-63, photograph page 66)

🚗 and 🚌 as 7a above. **30min on foot.** *Follow the notes for Short walk 7-4, page 65.* **Overlook a golden valley (at its best in summer) and the south coast. Some shade.**

8 PORTO NOVO FROM THE WEST (map pages 62-63, photo page 16)

🚗 or 🚌 2, etc to Assomada. By car, drive up the road on the east side of the church and its parking lot (Car tour 2). Bear left *and left again* (you can follow signposting to the 'Centro de Jardinagem'), to pass an electricity sub-station on your left. Just 1.1km uphill, there is a water trough on your right, raised up on pillars (an old mill-race). Park here, well tucked in. **10-15min on foot.** By bus, use notes for motorists above. **30-35min on foot.** *Follow the path at the left of the raised mill-race (tiled sign: 'Vereda Levada dos Moinhos') up to the Levada do Caniço, then turn right.* **You overlook the eastern escarpment of the valley and São Lourenço. The setting is ideal for an early evening picnic.**

10 LEVADA DA SERRA (map pages 62-63, photograph page 21)

🚗 or 🚌 77 to the Sítio das Quatro Estradas, where the ER202 joins the ER102. By car, head west towards Poiso and park by the levada after 0.5km, just past the piggery (Car tours 2, 4). **7min on foot.** By bus, follow Short walk 10-4, page 71. **22min on foot.** *Head north on the levada for about seven minutes.* **No far-reaching views, just a lovely setting.**

11 LEVADA DO CANIÇAL (map pages 80-81)

🚗 (Car tour 2) or 🚌 113 to the 'Pico do Facho' bus stop. Motorists should park at the start of the road to Pico do Facho, well tucked in. **20-30min on**

These rocks off the north coast of the Ponta de São Lourenço seem almost fluorescent (Car tour 2, Walk and Picnic 13)

foot. *Follow Short walk 11, page 72, for only 20-30min.* **Picnic on grassy verges in full sun, or in the shade of mimosas.**

13 ABRA BAY (map pages 76-77, photographs left and page 78) ○

🚗 (Car tour 2) or 🚌 113 to the Abra Bay viewpoint on São Lourenço Point (⌱), at the end of the ER109. **Up to 20min on foot.** *Picnic at the viewpoint or follow Walk 13 (page 76) for 15-20min.* **Magnificent coastal views, but no shade.**

15 PORTELA (map pages 80-81, photograph pages 82-83)

🚗 (Car tour 4) or 🚌 53 or 78 to Portela. **5min on foot.** *Follow Walk 15 (page 83) for 5min; if you like, continue further east along the track.* **Superb view over Penha de Águia, away from the coaches. Shade.**

16 LEVADA DO CASTELEJO (map pages 80-81, photo pages 84-85)

🚗 (Car tour 4) or 🚌 53 or 78 to Cruz. **Up to 30min on foot.** *Follow Walk 16 (page 84).* **You can look out towards Penha de Águia (20min) or up to the high peaks (25-30min). Shade nearby.**

19 PICO DO ARIEIRO (map on reverse of touring map, photograph pages 90-91) ○

🚗 Pico do Arieiro (Car tours 1, 4). **Up to 15min on foot.** *Picnic near the start of Walk 19, on a grassy verge before the first viewpoint (notes page 90).* **Stupendous mountain setting and views. No shade.**

20 ACHADA DO TEIXEIRA (map on reverse of touring map, photograph page 93)

🚗 Achada do Teixeira (Car tour 4). **5-50min on foot.** *Picnic at Homem em Pé (the basaltic dyke just below the house; 5min; shade), or follow Short walk 20 (page 92) to picnic on the Ruivo path or at Pico Ruivo itself (50min).* **Lacks the drama of Picnic 19, but the settings and views are fabulous.**

22 QUEIMADAS (map pages 98-99, photograph page 97)

🚗 Queimadas Park (accessible via a poorly surfaced narrow lane) or the Rancho Pico das Pedras on the ER218: see Car tour 4, 27. **Up to 35min on foot.** *Picnic by the Queimadas houses, or explore the Levada do Caldeirão Verde (see Short walks, page 97).* **No far-reaching views, but a fairytale setting.**

25 BALCÕES (map page 105, photograph page 28)

🚗 (Car tours 1, 4) or 🚌 56, 103 or 138 to Ribeiro Frio. **20min on foot.** *Follow the Short walk on page 104.* **Superb outlook over the central peaks, the Metade Valley and Fajã da Nogueira. Shade, bar-café nearby.**

26 PICO DA BONECA (map pages 98-99)

🚍 or 🚌 56, 103 or 138 to Cortado, just east of Santana (Car tours 1, 4). **25-30min on foot.** *Follow Short walk 1 on page 107; picnic at the trig point or on the contouring return path.* **Superb views over Santana and Faial. Adequate shade.**

27 ARCO DE SÃO JORGE (map page 110, photograph page 29)

🚍 (Car tours 1, 4) or 🚌 6 or 103 to the Snack Bar Arco on the ER101. **10-15min on foot.** *Take the beautifully cobbled trail at the left of the snack bar and follow it as long as you like.* **Brilliant views towards Boaventura and down over the sea from a sugar-loaf cliff.**

31 LOMBO DO MOURO (map on reverse of touring map, photographs page 116, similar views on pages 117, 119)

🚍 to the parking bay above the Lombo do Mouro house, signposted on the ER110 between Encumeada and Bica da Cana (Car tour 5). **10-15min on foot.** *Descend the steps to the house, then turn right a short way along the levada.* **Superb views east to the peaks and west to the escarpment of the Paúl da Serra; rushing levada; nearby shade.**

32 LEVADA DO NORTE, ENCUMEADA (map on reverse of touring map, nearby photograph page 117, right)

🚍 or 🚌 6 to Encumeada. Park at the viewpoint on the north side of the pass (Car tours 1, 5). **5-15min on foot.** *Climb steps opposite the bar/restaurant on the south side of the pass, to join the Levada do Norte (signposted 'Folhadal'). Picnic anywhere beside the levada, before the first tunnel (14min).* **Wonderful views to the great peaks; wealth of vegetation on the levada. Shade nearby.**

33 BICA DA CANA (map on reverse of touring map, photograph page 119)

🚍 at the entrance (with two concrete pillars) to the house (Car tour 5). **Up to 10min on foot.** *Follow the track towards the Bica house and then up to the triangulation point/miradouro (no shade).* **Stupendous views of the great peaks. Plenty of shade in the surrounding area.**

34 NOSSA SENHORA DA BOA MORTE (map p. 120)

🚍 at the chapel (a detour on Car tour 6). **No walking or up to 20min on foot.** *Picnic just below the chapel, on grassy slopes, or walk on to Pico Vermelho (see map page 120).* **Idyllic settings in a little-visited corner of the island.**

From a pine-shaded bench below Prazeres, you look out towards some of the most fascinating coastal cliffs on the island (Walk and Picnic 40, detour Car tour 6).

The afternoon sun paints the eastern escarpment of the Porto Novo ravine the colour of burnished copper (Picnic 8).

35 and 36 LEVADA DO PAÚL/LEVADA DA BICA DA CANA
(map pages 124-125, photographs pages 122, 126-127) ○

🚗 by the levada, below the statue of Cristo Rei, 9km north of Canhas on the ER209 (Car tour 5). **Up to 45min on foot.** *Follow the Levada do Paúl to the west (Walk 35, page 122; no shade) or the Levada da Bica da Cana to the east (Walk 36, page 126; a lone pine provides shade). Suggested picnic spots are described in the walking notes.* **Fine views over the south coast, beside a mesmerising ribbon of levada.**

37a-e RABAÇAL (map pages 124-125, photograph page 129)

🚗 Rabaçal (Car tour 5). *The road to Rabaçal is closed. to cars.* You can park on the ER211, from where you can walk to Rabaçal in 30 minutes: see notes for Alternative walk 37-1, page 128; **torch essential**. **Up to 50min on foot** *from Rabaçal.* *There are five picnic choices: (a) by the Rabaçal houses; (b) a sun-trap below the houses, at the Rabaçal end of the tunnel (follow Short walk 37-2 down to the Levada das 25 Fontes and turn left); (c) far side of the tunnel, overlooking Calheta's valley (follow (b), then continue past the sun-trap and through the tunnel —* **torch essential***); (d) Risco waterfall (Short walk 37-1); (e) 25 Fontes (Short walk 37-2).* **All these settings are lovely and have ample shade.**

38 LEVADA DA RIBEIRA GRANDE (map pages 124-125)

🚗 at the parking area on the ER110, at the top of the road to Rabaçal (Car tour 5). **12min on foot.** *Follow Walk 38 (page 131) to the pretty little reservoir.* **No views, but a lovely shady setting on a hot day.**

39 BELOW PICO RUIVO DO PAÚL (map pages 124-125, photographs page 132)

🚗 at the junction of the ER110 to Bica da Cana and the road to Estanquinhos, by a small levada (Car tour 5). **Up to 20min on foot.** *Follow Walk 39 (page 132) for as long as you like.* **Beautiful views across the Paúl da Serra and its miniature 'red peak'. Plenty of shade.**

40 PRAZERES (map pages 134-135, photograph page 15)

🚗 or 🚌 80 or 142 to Prazeres. By car (detour on Car tour 6), park at the Hotel Jardim Atlántico. **10min on foot.** By bus, walk 2km down to the hotel. **40min on foot.** *From the hotel follow Walk 40 (page 133) for just over 10min.* **Dramatic views to the sea and the steeply terraced cliffs west of Prazeres.**

42 LEVADA DA CENTRAL DA RIBEIRA DA JANELA
(map page 137, photograph page 136)

🚗 or 🚌 80 to the levada (Car tour 5). See 'How to get there', page 136. **3-30min on foot.** *Use the notes for Walk 42 (page 137); picnic by the first filtration point (3min; 🏠) or the second (30min).* **Fantastic views of the great Janela Valley; picturesque levada. Good shade.**

☀ *Touring*

Car touring on the island is a real pleasure for us, thanks to the new roads and expressways. From Funchal we can now be on the Paúl da Serra in 45 minutes — a drive that used to take three hours! But touring will be less pleasant during the life of this Eighth edition. EU funding will dry up in 2006; in the meantime there is a frenzy of road-building. Expect some errors in our touring notes; all was chaos during the research, with no detailed base maps available — just overall schematic plans. Even *we* found ourselves on the wrong road!

Drive *patiently* too; you are unlikely to average more than about 20-30km/h. On the older roads *beware of pot-holes and, sometimes, very deep ditches at the sides.* Plan leisurely excursions if possible, with walking breaks to stretch your legs. **The best one-day excursion is Car tour 1; Car tours 4 and 5 make an ideal two-day programme.**

In the touring and walking notes we often refer to **road numbers**. *This is to help you with orientation when using our maps,* since at time of writing there is hardly any signposting of road numbers, although this should change in the future.

Our touring notes are brief: they include little history or information that can be found in a general guide. We concentrate instead on the 'logistics' of touring: times and distances, road conditions, getting to the best viewpoints at the right time of day, etc. Most of all, we emphasise possibilities for **walking** and **picnicking**. If you're picnicking or sharing a car with walkers, you should find the 🚗 symbols on the walking maps useful: these alert you to places where you can park near a walk. And *do* refer to these walking maps from time to time while touring — perhaps when you stop at a viewpoint; they contain far more information than the touring map.

The large fold-out touring map is designed to be held out opposite the touring notes. City exits correspond to those on the Funchal plan on pages 10-11. **Symbols** used in the text are explained in the map key, but only *isolated* hotels and restaurants are shown on the map, as there are many good hotels and restaurants all around the island.

Allow ample time for stops: our times include only short breaks at viewpoints labelled 🌄 in the notes. Calculate time for **detours** as well: places, picnics and walks shown in ( ) are only accessible via detours off the main route.

All motorists should read the Country code on page 8 and go quietly in the countryside. *Boa viagem!*

1 MADEIRA NORTH AND SOUTH

Funchal • Encumeada • São Vicente • (Porto Moniz) • Boaventura • Santana • Faial • Ribeiro Frio • Poiso • (Pico do Arieiro) • Monte • Funchal

*113km/70mi; 5-6 hours' driving **without detours** (add about 30km/19mi; 1h for the detour to Porto Moniz and 14km/9mi; 1h for the detour to Pico do Arieiro); take the nearest expressway exit from Funchal.*

On route: ⊼ around Vinháticos, Encumeada, Chão dos Louros, above Rosário, Feiteiras, Ponta Delgada, Boaventura, São Jorge, ER103 around Ribeiro Frio, Poiso, Pico do Arieiro; Picnics (see **P** symbol and pages 12-16): (2, 19, 22), 25, 26, 27, 32, (42); Walks (2), 5, (7), 10, 18, 20, 21, 22, (23, 24), 25, 26, 27, (28, 29), 31, 32, (42)

*If you have only one day to tour the island, then this is the circuit to do, **including the detours to Porto Moniz and Pico do Arieiro**. Leave Funchal **very** early in the morning; we've planned the tour so that you have the best views westwards in the morning and to the east in the afternoon. If, however, you have a car for several days, then do Car tours 4 and 5 **instead of** this long expedition. The roads are mostly good, but some stretches on the north coast are narrow and frequented by tour coaches; you may be forced to back up to let them pass.*

From Funchal take the expressway west (Via Rápida; ER101), quickly whizzing across the lovely 'winged' bridge over the Socorridos. Not far beyond the exit for Cabo Girão/Quinta Grande the road dives beneath Campanário's church in a tunnel and soon describes a breathtaking arc out over the coast on a long bridge. After Exit 2 for Campanário and a short tunnel you enter the final, long tunnel: keep in the *left-hand* lane as you near the end of it, to follow signposting for 'São Vicente' (17km). (The right-hand lane is the turn-off to Ribeira Brava down on the coast, 2km away.)

After a fairly straight run along a narrow canyon graced with poplars you come to a fork: keep left for 'S Vicente via Encumeada' (22km). Now the road begins its winding ascent in earnest. Beyond **Serra de Água** you pass several picnic areas (⊡⊼) and then the Pousada dos Vinháticos (▲ ⊡⊼), beautifully sited below a ridge — the aptly named Crista de Galo ('Cock's Comb'). Some 2.5km further uphill (past the Residencial Encumeada ▲), Walk 4 comes in along a track on the right. The snaking ascent ends at **Encumeada★**, just at the centre of the island (1004m/3293ft; 28km ✕). Park on the left at the far side of this pass (⊡⊼WC), from where there are spectacular views down to the north coast and up to the Paúl da Serra in the west and the high peaks to the east. Walk 31 can begin here; Walk 20 ends on the other side of the road. While you are here, *do* take the opportunity to see the great Levada do Norte, described on pages 117-118 (Walk 32 and **P**32); the steps are on the south side of the pass, opposite the bar/restaurant.

Then descend into São Vicente's welcoming valley (⊡⊼), past **Chão dos Louros**, a lovely laurel grove (⊼ with

Car tours 1 and 5, Walk 29: The graceful clock tower of Nossa Senhora de Fátima graces a hilltop in São Vicente's valley.

fireplaces). Soon you'll have good views (📷🍴) over Rosário's church and stream: in high summer the hayricks weave ribbons of gold into the tapestry of this emerald landscape. Beyond **Rosário** you find yourself in the settings shown above and on page 1. At a roundabout, ignore the first exit signed to São Vicente (via a tunnel); take the second exit, to stay on the old road. At **Feiteiras** (📷🍴) you pass the ER208 to 'Ginjas' and 'Lanço'. Walk 29 begins and ends 5km up this road, at the Levada da Fajã do Rodrigues.

Come into the carefully restored village of **São Vicente** (39km ✝🏔✕🖳⊕∩), a good place to take a break for morning coffee ... and to make a decision: are you going to try to fit in a detour to Porto Moniz? If it's now later than 10.00, you really don't have the time. If you *do* have time, use the notes for Car tour 5 on page 30.

On leaving São Vicente, look out for the chapel (✝) built into a hollowed-out rock south of the bridge. Then either turn left towards Porto Moniz or follow the main tour: turn right on the coastal ER101 (🏔✕). After passing through a tunnel, your attention will be drawn to the chequered pattern made by the heath tree hedges protecting the terraces from the fierce northerly winds. Most of the fields are planted with vines, but this is for table wine; the vines which yield the grapes for the fortified Madeira wines are grown in the south, around Estreito de Câmara de Lobos. The road takes you in shadow below menacing cliffs, before you skirt above the lava-fertile promontory of **Ponta Delgada** (46km 🏔✕🖳) and soar up to a viewpoint (📷🍴) over the village setting and headlands to the east.

Above Ponta Delgada, a short stretch of cobbled road and an old, narrow tunnel are a delightful reminder of bygone

19

days, when driving round the island was a spine-rattling experience. Then the road turns inland, leaving the awesome coast for the green-gold gentleness of the great **Boaventura** (49km ▲▲ ✕ ⊕) valley. Both versions of Walk 27 begin at the village church. Just past Boaventura there is a good viewpoint (📷🍴) on the left. At the head of the valley (🚏) a road may one day be built to Curral das Freiras, via Falca.

The bucolic pleasures of this valley are a foretaste of the whole unforgettable landscape between Boaventura and Santana. As the road returns to the coastal cliffs, the Snack Bar/Restaurante Arco (**P**27), on the left, marks the halfway point of spectacular Walk 27b. You pass above **Arco de São Jorge** (56km ⊕), decked out with vines and hedgerows and rainbows of flowers. The hillsides are cultivated almost down to the sea, along the sweeping curve (*arco*) of the bay. Climb past mossy cliffs and dark pines brightened by banks of agapanthus, to another *miradouro* (📷🍴) with fine views back to Ponta Delgada's seaside church and swimming pool. Adjacent to this viewpoint are the beautifully landscaped Cabanas rondavels (▲▲✕).

Soon turn left for 'Vigia'. Take the short detour left to the *vigia* (📷), a splendid viewpoint, then continue into **São Jorge** (67km ✝🚏⊕). The richest baroque church outside Funchal is on your right. Walk 18, which descends the stupendous trail shown on the cover, can end here. Turn left on rejoining the ER101: beyond a bridge, you pass a road up right to Ilha, where Walk 28 ends. Soon you come upon enticing views of **Santana★** (75km *i*▲▲✕🚏⊕✝ **P**26), where orchards and market gardens roll down to the sea. Walk 26 is a lovely countryside circuit around Santana. If you haven't brought a picnic, this is the best place to stop for lunch.

From Santana we take the *old road* to **Faial** and then the ER103 as far as Poiso; use the notes on pages 28 and 29 (Car tour 4). It's about two hours from Santana to Funchal and, hopefully, you will have time to walk to Balcões from **Ribeiro Frio** (Short walk 25) and drive to Arieiro from Poiso.

Past **Poiso** (100km *excluding* the detour to Arieiro), continue south to **Monte★** (108km ✝▲▲❀✕). Walk above the delightful gardens to the church of Our Lady of the Mount, where you can see the tiny poignant statue to Madeira's patron saint. From the bottom of the church steps (departure point for the famous toboggan rides), you could follow the agapanthus-banked lane to the left (past the Monte Palace Gardens ❀ and the Funchal cable car terminus), to Babosas Balcony (15 minutes return on foot). Here a lovely chapel looks out over the impressive bowl of Curral dos Romeiros in the João Gomes River valley. Walk 7 can begin here.

Now it's just 5km back to Funchal (113km).

2 EASTERN MADEIRA'S GENTLE CHARMS

Funchal • Camacha • Santo da Serra • Machico • Ponta de São Lourenço • Pico do Facho • Santa Cruz • Funchal

85km/53mi; 4 hours' driving; Exit A from Funchal (plan pages 10-11)

On route: ⊟ at São Lourenço Point, Santa Cruz; Picnics (see **P** symbol and pages 12-16): (7a-b), 8, (10), 11, 13; Walks 7-14

Roads are asphalted, but sometimes potholed and with deep ditches at the sides. Allow a full day, to make the most of São Lourenço Point.

Either follow 'Camacha' off the Via Rápida (Exit 13) or leave Funchal from Exit A (Rua Dr Manuel Pestana Júnior). In either case, keep following signs for Camacha. Just 200m beyond a sign indicating a right turn to 'S Gonçalo 2km' you pass a fairly large large electricity sub-station on your right: the road to the **Palheiro Gardens** (❀ ▲▲ ✕) is at the far side of the sub-station fence. Just 1km above the Palheiro

Levada da Serra (Picnic 10 and Walk 10)

junction, the ER102 crosses the Levada dos Tornos (Walk 7). Now the road runs below the Levada da Serra (Walk 10), which may be joined at various points. Continue (✗⌷) up to **Camacha★** (10km ⛰✗⌷⊕WC), the centre of Madeira's willowcraft industry. The village square, the Achada da Camacha, overlooks the magnificent Porto Novo Valley. Short walk 7-3 and Walk 8 both begin here in the square.

Passing market gardens, continue to the wooded heights of **Eira de Fora** (⌷). There is a view down right over the Levada dos Tornos, before you come to **Águas Mansas** (15km) and pass the junction of the ER206 south (*P*7a-b; photograph page 66). Access to Short walk 10-3 is via the road on your left, 100m past this turn-off. Then round a bend to enter the great Boaventura basin, another valley irrigated by the Tornos. At 19km pass the ER202 left to Poiso; our favourite stretch of the Levada da Serra begins not far up this road (*P*10; photograph page 21) and would take you to Portela (Short walk 10-4, followed by Short walk 10-5).

At 21km fork right on the ER212 into **Santo da Serra** (22km ❀⛰✗⌷), a wooded village with several fine *quintas*. Walk 9 starts here; Walk 10 could begin or end here. Beyond the church, ignore the first sharp left turn to Machico, but bear left at a Y-fork signposted to Santa Cruz; you skirt the golf course. Ignore the right turn beyond the clubhouse and continue downhill, in 0.6km passing a right turn to Água de Pena and the Capela dos Cardais, where Walk 9 can also start. Two viewpoints (📷) on this road afford superb perspectives on the flawless setting of emerald-green Machico Bay, Pico do Facho, and the sun-baked arm of São Lourenço Point.

From the second viewpoint, continue down to the ER101 and go left for **Machico★** (30km ✝⛰✗⌷⊕), Madeira's first settlement. Of particular interest are the Manueline church and the Chapel of Miracles. The latter, on the east side of the river, was founded in 1420 on the site of Zarco's first landfall; destroyed by a flood in 1803, the chapel was rebuilt later in the 19th century.

At time of writing, roads around Machico were in chaos; you want to continue on the *old road*, the ER109 to Caniçal.* Climbing the lush eastern flanks of Machico's valley (✗), you come to the Caniçal tunnel (*P*11), where Walk 11 ends; Walks 12 and 14 and Short walk 11 begin here. Beyond a pretty line of palm trees fanning out above the grassy slopes, turn down right into **Caniçal** (38km ✗ and whaling **M**), a

---

*But if you are taking walkers to the start of Walk 11, follow signs for 'Porto da Cruz'. Drive along the left-hand side of the Machico River and go through a first tunnel. Just at the exit, turn right and then immediately left. Bar Fonte Vermelha is just on your left. From here make your way to the ER109 by using the map on pages 80-81.

There are superb views over the Bay of Funchal from Pináculo, an aloe-spiked promontory above São Gonçalo. What a stupendous view of the fireworks the nearby hotel must have on New Year's Eve!

once-poor fishing port now bursting its seams with new buildings as a result of the adjacent tax-free industrial zone.

From here return to the main road and continue straight out (🏔️ 🍴) to **São Lourenço Point**★. Use the notes on pages 76-78 to explore; perhaps picnic at Abra Bay (44km 📷🎍*P*13; Walk 13) or one of the viewpoints (📷🎍).

On your return from the point, turn left on the far side of the Caniçal tunnel to **Pico do Facho** (53km 📷), to admire the view over Machico and its harbour, nestling below the hills of Santo da Serra. Continuing west (🍴), follow 'Funchal' on the ER101, driving between the massive pillars supporting the airport runway. Just beyond the airport, turn right at Exit 21 for 'Santa Cruz (este)'. Coming onto the old coastal road, turn left into delightful **Santa Cruz**★ (64km ⛪🏔️🍴🚻). Here you can stretch your legs in the *til*-shaded square and visit the bright-white church of São Salvador, one of the finest Manueline buildings on the island and the largest church outside Funchal. The lido, with its cafés, palms and pebble beach, is a pleasant place to relax.

Leaving Santa Cruz, go through an underpass below the ER101, following signs for Gaula at first. Then ignore the turn-off right for Gaula; follow 'Funchal'. Just after crossing the great cleft of the Porto Novo Valley, turn off right and then go left for Assomada. Short walk 8 begins at **Assomada**'s church (*P*8). Turn left down to **Caniço** (75km *i*⛪🏔️🍴🚌🚻), a major tourist centre. After visiting the church, head back north to the ER204, quickly coming to **Cançela** (78km 🍴🚌). *Carefully follow signposting for São Gonçalo,* keeping in the left-hand lane in order to join the narrow old road hugging the coast *(ignore the turn-off right for the Via Rápida here).* Some 2km along, pull over left at the viewpoint shown above (📷). Then take advantage of the inevitable traffic jam in **São Gonçalo** (🍴🚌) to admire the fine old houses on the eastern outskirts of Funchal, before regaining the centre (85km).

3 THE CORRAL AND THE CAPE

Funchal • Pico dos Barcelos • Eira do Serrado • Curral das Freiras • Câmara de Lobos • Cabo Girão • Funchal

64km/40mi; 3 hours' driving; Exit B from Funchal (plan pages 10-11)

On route: ⊞ on the ER107 to Curral, Cabo Girão; Picnic (see *P* symbol and pages 12-16): 3; Walks 3, (4, 6). (Walk 1 is near this tour, but is best reached direct from Funchal by bus.)

For the best light, do this short tour in the afternoon. The ER107 to Curral das Freiras, although steep and winding, is well built-up at the sides.

Either take Exit 8 for 'P dos Barcelos' off the Via Rápida or leave Funchal by Exit B (the statue to Freedom in front of Reid's Gardens, signposted 'Estádio'). Leaving from Exit B, you very soon pick up signposting for Pico dos Barcelos. As you approach the slender spire of São Martinho's church, on a hill, turn right, cross the expressway, and continue to **Pico dos Barcelos**★ (6km ✕⌾WC), a tree-shaded *miradouro* offering fine views over Funchal and the east.

Continue north, now following signposting to the Eira do Serrado. The ER107 climbs through forests of eucalyptus and pine splintered by golden sun-shafts (✕⊞). Ignore the tunnel direct to Curral; keep left on the old road. A good viewpoint (⌾) over the Socorridos ravine is passed on the left, before you reach the right-hand fork to the **Eira do Serrado**★ (18km ▲⌾WC*P*3). No doubt you will join the crowds and climb the paved path to the main viewpoint, from where there are stupendous views over Curral, 400m/1300ft below. But to hug all this splendour to yourself, follow Walk 3 from the 15min-point (page 47) for five to ten minutes. Better still, do *all* of Walk 3, then take a bus back to your car!

Beyond the Eira the road winds down and through two tunnels into the crater-like ravine where **Curral das Freiras**★ (the 'Nuns' Corral'; 22km ✕WC; photograph pages 46-47) huddles below awesome heights. Curral is a famous walkers' 'crossroads': Walks 3 and Alternative walk 20 end near the village, and experts could begin or end Walk 4 here. It has long been planned to extend the ER107 from here to Boaventura in the north, but work seems to have come to a standstill.

Return the same way (or via the tunnel) and, 1km past Pico dos Barcelos (just before São Martinho Church), turn right, to get on the expressway west. After crossing the Socorridos, take Exit 5 for **Câmara de Lobos**★ (*i*✕⊕ and ♦ founded by Zarco in 1424). Follow the one-way system down to the centre (car park). When you've looked at the colourful fishing boats and the church, leave on the road signposted 'CTT Correos'. As you make the sharp left turn back to the main road (ER229 ☝), a plaque above a terrace on the right alerts you to the place where Sir Winston Churchill painted the curving white arc of the village against the backdrop of

From the top of Cabo Girão, safe behind iron railings, you can marvel at the toy ships at sea some 580m/1900ft below you … and at the tenacity of the sure-footed Madeiran farmers working their tiny terraces.

the awesome red cape, Cabo Girão. Continuing west on the ER229 (🚌), turn right just over 1.5km uphill, to climb to **Pico da Torre** (📷), a lovely viewpoint over Câmara de Lobos.

The road winds below **Estreito de Câmara de Lobos** (44km ✕⊕), where the grapes for the island's fortified wines are grown*, and an exceptionally gorgeous display of terraced vineyards pours down the hillsides below **Garachico**'s church (photograph page 57).** Turn left to **Cabo Girão★** (51km *i*🅿📷WC), where Short walk 6-1 can end. From this sea-cliff you enjoy the spectacular view shown above. But if you are a keen walker, your eyes will be drawn to the 'winged' bridge over the Socorridos and then up the valley to the mountains.

From here return to Funchal on the expressway (64km).

*__Detour 1__ (either 8.5 or 14km return; see map pages 54-55): Turn right into Estreito, curl left round the church, then drive straight uphill. Just beyond a chapel on the left (0.7km past the church), you cross the Levada do Norte (Walk 6). At a fork (1.6km) keep left for 'Foro' and 'Jardim da Serra'. Ignore a road on the right (3.4km) and curve round left over a bridge. Almost immediately, bear right at a Y-fork (keeping the 'Central da Pereira' on your left). This area is called **Jardim da Serra** (Garden in the Mountains). The hotel you pass on the left (4.2km; 🏨) was once a lovely old *quinta*, built in the 1800s by the English consul, Henry Veitch. From here he sent fruit, books and old wines to Napoleon, when the Northumberland laid anchor in Funchal on its passage to St Helena. From the hotel you can continue uphill for another 2.5km to the end of the road: **Boca da Corrida**, the superb viewpoint where Walk 4 begins and Alternative walk 5 nears its end.
**__Detour 2__ (8km return): Just after Garachico you pass a road off left to the Via Rápida. You can follow this road all the way to the coastal cliffs, where there is a cable car down to Fajã das Bebras, a landslip just east of Cabo Girão. As you approach Junction 4 of the Via Rápida, a small sign on the right (*'Fajãs teleférico'*) points the way. Map pages 54-55.

25

4 MOUNTAINS AND MORE MOUNTAINS!

Funchal • Poiso • Pico do Arieiro • Portela • Porto da Cruz • Achada do Teixeira • Santana • (São Jorge • Arco de São Jorge) • Faial • Ribeiro Frio • Funchal

*141km/88mi; about 6-7 hours' driving, **excluding** the detour to Arco de São Jorge; Exit A from Funchal (plan pages 10-11)*

On route: ᚠ at Poiso, Pico do Arieiro, ER202 west of the Levada da Serra, ER108 north of Portela, ER103 around Ribeiro Frio, Pico das Pedras, ER218 to Achada do Teixeira, path to Pico Ruivo, Queimadas Park; Picnics (see **P** symbol and pages 12-16): 2, 10, 15, 16, 19, 20, (22), 25, 26, (27); Walks: 2, 7, 9, 10, 14-21, (22-24), 25, 26, (28)

*It is usual to include the mountainous northeast of the island in what is often called a 'Santana Tour', covering all of central Madeira (our Car tour 1). We find this very hectic and urge you to devote an entire day to visiting the great rugged peaks and the gentle moorland roads radiating from Poiso Pass. This tour fits in nicely with Car tour 5, providing a leisurely two-day introduction to many of Madeira's best landscapes. Start out early in the morning and **aim to reach Arieiro no later than 09.30**; clouds often descend by about 10.00. If you do not plan to take any short walks, you will have time to go further west than Santana — to São Jorge (18km return; 1h) or possibly Arco (38km return; 2h) — a part of the island not to be missed. Although this tour is long, the roads are all good, although winding and occasionally potholed.*

The direct route to Arieiro from Funchal is Exit C (Rua 31 de Janeiro; ER103), via Monte. But we suggest you try another way: leave as for Car tour 2 and use the notes on page 21 past the road to the **Palheiro Gardens** (5km). In a minute more, the ER201 joins from the left. Turn up left here and follow this pine- and eucalyptus-shaded road northwest. You cross the Levada dos Tornos (Walk 7) and pass the cobbled trail where Walk 10 begins. Some 2.7km further on, there is a fine *miradouro* on the left, looking out over Curral dos Romeiros. At **Terreiro da Luta★** (14km ✝✖️🖼WC) a statue to Our Lady of Peace commemorates the sufferings of the people of Funchal during World War I. At the base of the statue there is a rosary made from the anchor chains of ships torpedoed in Funchal harbour. In the early 1900s a luxurious cog railway climbed up here via Monte. The views over the city's setting are superb, but soon you must press on! Join the ER103 ahead and turn right.* The road, lined with hydrangeas and agapanthus, snakes its way up past the Montado do Pereiro (Δ) to a barren plateau and then **Poiso Pass** (1400m/4600ft; 20km ✖️ᚠ🖼).

Here turn left on the highland road (ER202) to **Pico do**

*Some 3km beyond Terreiro da Luta, at the Montado do Barreiro forestry house, you will pass two roads on the left. The first goes to a viewpoint at Pico Alto (ᚠ) and the second (open daily from 08.00 to 19.00) climbs all the way to the Pico do Arieiro road. While most maps indicate a through road, you *cannot* get to Arieiro this way (there is a cul-de-sac sign at the entrance). A locked gate bars access to the ER202. But *do* explore this beautiful forestry road (ᚠ) when you have the time.

Arieiro★ (1818m/5963ft; 27km ☐☒WC***P**19; Walk 19; photograph pages 90-91). The once-popular *pousada* is now closed; we have been told that a NATO base will be built here sometime in the future. Before leaving, be sure to visit the **Miradouro do Juncal** (☒ 15min return; the path begins on the east side of the road): from here you have fine views over the sweep of the Metade Valley down to Faial and Penha de Águia ('Eagle Rock'). Later in the day, you will have another 'eagle's eye' view of the Metade, from Balcões.

On your return, watch for the ice house hidden below the road on your right, some 2km below the peak ('Poço da Neve'; ***P**2; photograph page 13). Walk 2 starts here. Then pass the meteorological station and come again to **Poiso** (34km). Now go straight ahead on the ER202 opposite, a beautiful moorland road. Overlooking the reservoir *(lagoa)* at Santo da Serra, you descend past shaded ☐ and then cross the Levada da Serra (***P**10; photograph page 21). You meet the ER102 at the Sítio das Quatro Estradas ('place where four roads join'; 42km); Walk 9 and Short walk 10-3 end here; Short walk 10-4 begins here. Turn left, passing the ER212 into Santo da Serra (☒) and continuing north to **Portela★** (49km ☒☒***P**15), where Walk 25 ends and Walk 15 begins. Here you enjoy the superb view to the north coast shown on pages 82-83, with Penha de Águia dominating the landscape.

From Portela take the ER108 north (☒☐). Alternative walk 16, through a valley called 'Hold on; watch you don't fall!', begins at **Referta** (52.5km). At a roundabout, be sure to follow signs to **Porto da Cruz** (55km ☒☒⊕), where Walks 14 and 15 end. *Always keeping to the old ER108,* you pass a good viewpoint (☒) back over the village as you climb west to skirt the towering mass of Eagle Rock. Don't blink, or you might miss **Cruz** (57km; ***P**16), where Walk 16 begins and the descent from Eagle Rock ends (Walk 17). Just before crossing the bridge over the Ribeira de São Roque, turn right (signposted '**Penha de Águia**'). Walk 17 begins 1.1km uphill, at the Restaurante Galé (☒). Continue to a turning circle at the end of the road, from where there is a fine view (☒) towards Faial and up to Pico do Arieiro. Return, cross the bridge and pass the ER103 on your left (60km ☒). Skirt the centre of **Faial** (☒⊕) and, avoiding the tunnel, keep to the old road, to make for Santana — for the present ignoring the two roadside viewpoints. The sun is now too high for this landscape to be seen at its best.

With good planning you will reach the Santana area late in the morning. Before coming to the village centre, turn left on the ER218 for 'Pico das Pedras/Pico Ruivo'. Climb to the crossing of the Levada do Caldeirão Verde at the Rancho Pico das Pedras (▲☒). Walk 21 and Short walk 21 both

The high peaks and the Fajã da Nogueira Valley from Balcões

begin here. Some 250m further uphill you come to the **Pico das Pedras** forestry house (with fireplaces). Beyond two well-sited viewpoints, one of them involving a stiff climb, the road ends on a plateau. This is the **Achada do Teixeira** (79km), where Walk 19 ends and Walk 20 begins. You could picnic here (*P*20) at Homem em Pé (photograph page 93) or on the Ruivo path. Or you might like to walk to Queimadas* (*P*22); if so, park by the Rancho Pico das Pedras.

Turn back to **Santana**★ (93km *P*26), where Walk 18 begins and Walk 22 ends. Circular Walk 26 is a tour around Santana, taking in the most spectacular views. The village is an enchantment of patchwork-quilt gardens and orchards set below mountains. Break for lunch here, if you didn't bring a picnic. Then decide whether to press on to São Jorge () or Arco (), returning the same way. You want to leave Santana at about 15.00.

Return to Faial, again on the old road. It's now afternoon, and you are just in time to enjoy the best views from the two *miradouros* () west of the village or, lower down, the Fortim do Faial off to the left. Clouds scud across the sky, creating fascinating mosaics of light and shade on this dramatic landscape. Eagle Rock is seen from base to summit, standing guard over church and village, at the confluence of three great river valleys: the Metade, the Seca and the São Roque. This superb panorama is likely to be one of your most lasting impressions of Madeira.

*1.3km west of the ER218, a *very* narrow, poorly surfaced lane with few passing places climbs steeply to Queimadas (Walks 22, 23 and 28). It's usually easier to walk from the Rancho Pico das Pedras (30 minutes each way), unless you're lucky enough to find the lane newly tarred.

Two walks from Boaventura: the Levada de Cima (Walk 27a) and Arco de São Jorge's sugarloaf cliff (Walk 27b)

Beyond **Faial** turn right on the ER103 (✕). Look left to see São Roque atop its *lombo* (the spine separating the parallel ravines of the São Roque and Metade rivers), as you follow the road up the spectacularly terraced Seca Valley towards the mountains shown in silhouette on pages 84-85. Walk 21 ends at **Cruzinhas** (105km), in a magnificent splurge of cultivation (photograph page 96).

Just after you cross the Metade, pass a rough road right to the power station at Fajã da Nogueira (Walk 24). Climb past the fruit trees of **Achada do Cedro Gordo** and forests of cedar, cypress, pine and eucalyptus (⊼). Beyond a viewpoint (📷) left over the Ribeiro Frio Valley, you reach the sweet coolness of **Ribeiro Frio★** (111km ✕⊼❀◄).

Take a break here to walk to Balcões (Short walk 25, page 104). From these 'Balconies' (📷*P*25) you have a view to contrast with that from the Juncal *miradouro* visited earlier in the day. Eagle Rock is seen again, presiding over the north coast villages. But from the Balcões the jagged central peaks dominate the scene. The Metade takes its source on these heights, and its tributaries feed the power station 250m/800ft below you (Walk 24), from where the Tornos Levada flows on to irrigate the southeast.

Beyond the trout hatcheries and small botanical garden, wind uphill (⊼) through conifers, back to **Poiso** (118km). Just 0.5km south of the pass, turn left on the ER203 signposted to Camacha. Light industries are steadily encroaching on this old moorland road. When you lose the moorland to gorse, ferns and pine, you cross the Levada da Serra at Paradise Valley (Short walk 10-2). Half a kilometre further on, meet the ER102 (✕) and turn right, back to Funchal (141km).

5 PORTO MONIZ AND THE PAÚL DA SERRA

Funchal • São Vicente • Seixal • Ribeira da Janela • Fanal • Porto Moniz • (Achadas da Cruz) • Ribeira da Janela Valley • Paúl da Serra • Bica da Cana • Encumeada • Funchal

*149km/92mi; 5 hours' driving, **excluding** the detour to the cable car at Achadas da Cruz; take the Via Rápida west from Funchal.*

On route: ⌂ at Vinháticos, Encumeada, Chão dos Louros, above Rosário, Feiteiras, Porto Moniz, Fonte do Bispo, Rabaçal, Bica da Cana; Picnics (see **P** symbol and pages 12-16): 31-33, (35-37), 38, 39, (42); Walks: 20, (29), 31-33, (35-37), 38, 39, (42). The 'Appetizer' walk described on page 41 is also en route, and a short walk or picnic in the Fanal is *highly recommended*.

This is the most beautiful tour to the west and combines especially well with Car tour 4, to provide a two-day programme covering almost all of Madeira's best landscapes. If you've already done Car tour 1, you could save some time by using the Encumeada tunnel.

Follow Car tour 1 to **São Vicente** (39km ⛪🏔✕🚌⊕∩). North of the village, turn left for Porto Moniz. Much of the route runs through tunnels, but from this direction you can still follow parts of the one-way 'Antiga ER101'. If you are only going to detour onto this old road once, then take the third turn-off; this stretch affords the best opportunity of savouring the thrill of the old corniche route, with its waterfalls and spectacular coastal views.

Be sure to turn off right to **Seixal** (46km 🏔✕⊕), where the church perches high above the coast. Notice the steep vineyards here, edged with feathery heath tree fencing. If you haven't brought a picnic, there is a superb fish restaurant down by the sea (follow 'Cais'). Not far past Seixal, a road signposted 'Praia' leads to a pleasant seaside promenade.

Continue on the coastal road west towards Ribeira da Janela: village and river take their name from the 'window' *(janela)* in the 'sea-horse' rock just off the coast. Not far past a (perhaps still derelict) fish farm (just beyond a tunnel and *before* a bridge and power station), turn off left for 'Ribeira da Janela, Fanal'. Keeping right at a junction and always climbing, you pass below the village church at **Ribeira da Janela**. Some 12km uphill, turn left on a road signposted as a cul-de-sac (just before a sign pointing ahead to the Paúl da Serra). Keep left at a fork almost immediately, then park just before a chained-off trail. The **Fanal★** forestry house (65km) is just ahead to the right. Follow the old trail past the forestry house and into a wonderland of centuries-old *til* trees (the laurels shown on page 8). This is a wonderful area to stretch your legs and picnic.

Return the same way, enjoying a fine view back east along the coast and down over the *janela* rock on the descent. Back on the coastal road, turn left over the bridge, pass the power station and go under the pipe carrying water from the reservoir where Walk 42 begins. Soon you're in **Porto Moniz★** (79km *i*🏔△🍴🍷⊕🚌WC), where natural lava-rock pools have been beautifully incorporated into an extensive swimming complex with good facilities. The 'Appetizer' walk on page 41 ends here, having descended the sheer coastal cliffs behind the village.

Climb out of Porto Moniz on steep hairpin bends, past two bird's-eye viewpoints (📷) over the village setting. Just 3.5km up from the roundabout by the petrol station, you pass the road off left to Walk 42 (*P*42), signposted to Lamaceiros. The 'Appetizer' walk mentioned above begins 100m before the church in **Santa**; it's a very steep, but technically easy descent to Porto Moniz. Beyond Santa the main tour turns left on the ER110 for Funchal at the cattle market (85km). *Detour:* First you could make a detour of 12km return to the cable car near Achadas da Cruz (🚠): keep ahead to the signpost 'Miradouro, Teleférico', then turn right. Even if you don't take the hair-raising ride, the view straight down to Quebrada Nova, 640m/2100ft below, is breathtaking.

The ER110 at first runs southeast, high above Madeira's greatest ravine. The far-off views over the north and south coasts are splendid. But even more impressive is the size and magnificence of the **Janela Valley**. Virgin forests of heath and laurel cloak the mountainsides like green sable.

Our first stop is at the ruined 'Casa do Elias' at **Quebradas** (90km 📷), from where there is a superb view over Ribeira da Janela on its conical hilltop. Soon come to another *miradouro* near **Fonte do Bispo** (96km 📷🚌), from where the ER210 runs south down to Prazeres. If you have binoculars, looking southeast you can see the Rabaçal houses at the head

Paúl da Serra

of the valley … and even the Risco waterfall. Across the valley you can see the old laurels on the Fanal hillsides. Beyond the Fanal, the peaks in the east rise above cloud necklaces. The lighthouse at Ponta do Pargo is glimpsed in the west.

At 103km, you pass the ER211 south to Calheta. The much-loved beauty spot, Rabaçal (🚐**P**37a-e; Walk 37) is most easily reached from a parking spot 2km down this road, *but you need a torch* (see page 128). Soon you reach the head of the valley, by a reservoir and parking bay (📷**P**38 and Walk 38; photograph page 131). Here you are just above Rabaçal, but the road is closed to traffic. It's an easy stroll down, but a very tiring ascent of 2km (200m/650ft) back up.

Past the Pico da Urze (▲▲) you are on the **Paúl da Serra**, so very different from the Janela Valley. Even in winter rain the Paúl has a strange beauty: the moors take on a golden hue, the bracken throws up wine-red flames, and seagulls swirl over the marshes. On sunny days, the air is bright as diamonds. Beyond the signpost left 'Fanal/Ribeira da Janela', you come to the ER209 south: Walks 35 and 36 begin 4km down this road (**P**35, 36). Turn left for Bica da Cana, passing a statue to Nossa Senhora da Serra on the right. Walk 39 (photographs page 132) begins at the signpost left to 'Estan-quinhos' (**P**39). But keep *right* here for **Bica da Cana**: two concrete pillars mark the stone-laid trail to this old hunting lodge, on your left (111.5km 🚻 and 📷 at the end of the track above the house; **P**33 and Walk 33).

Continue on the ER110 for the breathtaking descent to Encumeada. You look out to the high peaks in the east, the landscape shown on page 119. Some 4.5km from Bica, a signpost on the right, 'Lombo do Mouro', alerts you to the refuge shown on page 116 (**P**31 and Walk 31). Just over 1km further on, Alternative walk 33 begins its climb to Pináculo. Soon you skirt above the magnificent Rabaças and Norte levadas and follow them to **Encumeada★** (121km 📷🚻✕). From here retrace your outgoing route to Funchal (149km).

On the descent from Santa to Porto Moniz ('Appetizer' walk described on page 41)

6 THE SUNNY SOUTHWEST COAST

Funchal • Ribeira Brava • Prazeres • Ponta do Pargo • Achadas da Cruz • Fajã da Ovelha • Paúl do Mar • Jardim do Mar • Calheta • Ponta do Sol • (Ribeira Brava) • Funchal

147km/91mi; 6 hours' driving; Exit D from Funchal (plan pages 10-11)

On route: ♒ at Campanário, Ponta do Sol, Arco da Calheta, Prazeres, east of Raposeira; Picnics (see **P** symbol and pages 12-16): (6, 34, 40); Walks (5), 6, 30, 31, 34, 35, 40, 41

This tour follows inland roads all the way west — for the views and the walks. We then return by the shorter coastal road and the expressway.

Leave Funchal by Exit D, passing the heavily built-up hotel area along the coast. Beyond Câmara de Lobos (Car tour 3), the ER229 winds below **Estreito de Câmara de Lobos** (✕⊕; Walk 6) and **Garachico**. Just 0.8km past the left turn to **Cabo Girão★** the road crosses the Levada do Norte at **Quinta Grande** (Short walk 6-2).* And 3km past the petrol station at the end of **Campanário** (✕⏢⊕♒) a road on the right signposted 'S João, S Paulo, Levada do Norte' leads to Boa Morte (**P**6) and Fontes (Walk 5). Soon you're circling steeply down into **Ribeira Brava★** (31km *i*▲✕⏢⊕M and ♁ founded in the 1500s), where Walks 30 and 31 end. The Museu Etnológico is well worth a visit.

Turn right inland off the esplanade for 'S Vicente' and, *almost immediately, turn left over a bridge,* to climb the ER222. After about 8km Lombada da Ponta do Sol (♁) is signposted up to the right; a detour to the village would take you to the beautiful old manor *(solar)* visited on Walk 30. Just beyond the church in **Canhas** (43km ✝✕) notice the first of the 14 Stations of the Cross on your right; after the last, on a straight stretch of road (⏢), there is a monument to St Theresa (✝). (Nearby is the taxi rank, if you are dropping off passengers for Walks 35-37). Not far along, the ER209 heads up right to the Paúl da Serra. Soon you come to two dramatic viewpoints (☞♒) straight down over the sparkling houses and banana trees of Madalena do Mar, 450m/1500ft below.

At **Arco da Calheta** you pass a road up right to Pico do Arco (☞✕), where there is another splendid viewpoint over Madalena do Mar. Walk 35 ends on the western outskirts of Arco, at **Loreto**. The Manueline church here (♁) demands a visit, if you are lucky enough to catch the key-holder on site.

Climb under mimosa to **Prazeres** (67km ▲♒), where Walk 40 begins. A detour left to the hotel would take you to a splendid viewpoint over Paúl do Mar, 600m/2000ft below

---

*From the turn-off to Junction 3 on the expressway you can have an amazing experience: follow signs for *'Elevador'*. A lift with windows will drop you almost 300m/1000ft straight down the cliffs west of Cabo Girão — to Fajã dos Padres, an idyllic stony beach and plantation (✕). You'll want to spend the day, so save this detour of about 4km for another day. This landslip is only accessible by lift or boat.

'Esmeraldo's domain', near Lombada da Ponta do Sol (Walk 30)

(☞*P*40; photograph page 15). Walk 41, along the photogenic levada shown on page 135, starts just below the church at **Raposeira**. Soon you pass the turn-off left to Faja da Ovelha (72km ᛘ). For the moment, keep ahead to **Ponta do Pargo** (81km), the base for circular Walk 34. Follow 'Farol'; this road (▲▲) takes you to the lighthouse★ (83km ☜) the most westerly point on Madeira. Past the lighthouse, the road continues to a viewpoint and tea house/restaurant (☜✕). The ongoing road here leads straight back to Ponta do Pargo's church, but it soon becomes cobbled and very narrow, so you may prefer to go back the way you came.

Back on the ER101, turn right* and retrace your route east for 9km, then turn right on the ER223 (ᛘ) to **Faja da Ovelha**. Continue south (☜) to seaside **Paúl do Mar** (104km ✕), where Walk 40 ends. Passing to the left of the church, bear left for Jardim do Mar, going into a tunnel. At the end of the tunnel, turn right into beautifully restored **Jardim do Mar** (✕), where you can wander the pretty cobbled paths.

Leaving Jardim do Mar, return to the tunnel exit and turn right for Calheta. At the next fork, again turn right for 'Calheta, Funchal'. Just 1km further on, keep straight ahead into a tunnel (signposting: 'Riu Bartolomeu'). Beyond an adjacent tunnel, bear right towards 'Estrela' but, at the T-junction, go left for 'Calheta, Ribeira Brava'. At **Calheta** (♙▲▲✕☭⊕☜) you descend past the church on the right (notice that it has been cut back to accommodate the road!) and then a power station. Coming onto the seafront promenade, there is a pretty viewpoint on the right and the restored remains of an old *aguardente* (sugar cane spirit) factory a short way along to the left. At a T-junction beyond the hotel, where Arco is signposted up to the left, keep right for Funchal.

The restored cottages at the far end of **Madalena do Mar** are the most attractive part of this seaside village (note the poignant shrine in the nearby wall). More tunnels now carry you to **Ponta do Sol** (123km ✕☭⊕ᛘ and ♙ founded in the 15th century), where elegant façades grace another seaside promenade. Curve left uphill out of the village and, at a fork, *keep ahead* for Funchal. At the roundabout, take the first exit, immediately going through another tunnel. **Lugar de Baixo** is reputed to be the sunniest place on Madeira. Following signs for Funchal, you can bypass busy Ribeira Brava and pick up the Via Rápida back to Funchal (147km).

*Or first detour left to the Boa Morte chapel (*P*34; see map page 120).

☀ Walking

Over 100 long and short walks are described in this Eighth edition, but you can devise many more for yourself, covering the length and breadth of the island. Most of our walks are linear because they follow old trails and the levadas. If you have hired a car, don't be discouraged by the lack of circular walks. *Take the time to plan ahead: study the maps and the bus timetables.* You can use your car and the buses (or taxis) in tandem. Remember that all the walks are keyed into the car tours, and the best access routes and parking details are given where relevant.

Beginners: Many walks are suitable for you. Start with those described as easy, and be sure to check all the short and alternative walks — some are easy versions of the longer walks. Look, too, at the picnic suggestions.

Experienced walkers: If you are accustomed to rough terrain and have a head for heights, you should be able to take most of the walks in this book in your stride. Provided, of course, that storm damage or bulldozing has not made the way unsafe, and *provided that you follow the route as we describe it.* If you have not reached one of our landmarks after a reasonable time, you must go back to the last 'sure' point and start again.

Experts: You should manage all the walks easily, *provided that you are used to very sheer unprotected drops* (some levada paths give virtually no respite from constant 'exposure'). We've also alerted you to some other walks you might like to tackle.

It is important that *all* walkers, whether beginners or experts, read and *heed* the Country code on page 8.

G uides, waymarking, maps

Quite a few of our routes edge sheer drops and are potentially dangerous; under 'Grade' we say that you must be sure-footed and have a head for heights. Until you get used to Madeira's terrain and know your 'vertigo tolerance', why not try one of these walks with a **guided group**? Several firms now operate inexpensive minibus tours with guides throughout the year; enquire at the Tourist Office.

During the late 1990s several routes were **signposted** and a few **waymarked** with red and yellow flashes (two horizontal stripes mean *continue this way*; X means *do not go this way*). We will refer to these waymarks where they existed at time of writing. The plan is to eventually waymark *all* island walks.

no danger

some danger

very dangerous!

★ flat or slight ascent/descent

★★ moderate ascents/descents

★★★ very strenuous

Example: no danger, but

★★ some effort required

You may also come upon some old, simple star- and colour-coded signs erected by the Regional Forestry Commission for the benefit of Madeirans who like to walk. The colour refers to the potential danger and the stars to the effort required. ***We do not always agree with their gradings!***

Our walking **maps** are based on the latest 1:50,000 two-sheet map of the island published in 1995 by the Instituto Geográfico e Cadastral* and our own research on foot or by car. We have enlarged our maps to a scale of 1:40,000 to include a bit more detail, but the only paths shown on our maps are those we know to be viable *at time of writing,* even if they not described in the book. (For example, we show the footpaths in the Serra das Funduras near Portela and the path from Boca dos Namorados to Curral.) ***Note that some of the paths we show are very difficult or vertiginous; unless you are an expert, please stick to the walks described (those highlighted with solid or dashed green lines).***

Where to stay

If you have only a week on the island, or if walking is not your top priority, it's best to stay in **Funchal**. The bus network radiates from the capital. But the good news for keen walkers is that there is now ***good hotel accommodation all over the island — in villages and in the mountains***, more frequent bus services, and more fly-drive packages than ever before. Judicious use of the bus timetables — together with a hired car, if you so choose — will take you to a good selection of walks *wherever* you are based. Ask your nearest Portuguese Tourist Office for the Madeira accommodation guide, or check the web: www.madeiratourism.org.

Our walks pass by several 'rest houses' in Madeira's mountains. These are for the use of government officials, school parties, etc — not for foreign visitors (although you will be welcome to picnic in the grounds).

The only **camping sites** are at Porto Moniz and Montado do Pereiro. Check the web: www.madeira-camping.com.

*This map should be available from your local map specialist. But be warned: it highlights *roads and tracks;* few paths are shown. The roads are now very out of date, and although the sheets were designed for reproduction at a scale of 1:50,000 they are almost impossible to use 'on the ground', because paths and tracks are printed in pale grey.

Weather

Madeira has fine walking weather all year round, although summer is most reliable (and usually not too hot). Equinoctial rains can be expected in spring and autumn, but there will be many fine days as well. We tend to avoid June and early July, however, as the island is often covered by a 'hood' of low-lying clouds (the *capacete*).

Safe walking demands accurate reading of the weather signs and common sense. Outside summer many walks, especially in the north and west, can be treacherous. Even on the most glorious winter's day, levada paths will be full to overflowing and some mountain trails like waterfalls. *Never forget that anywhere on the island, at any time of year, a landslide can wipe out a path overnight.*

Apart from the seasons, Madeira's weather is determined by **wind direction**. Whatever the season, the weather will be at its best with a light northeasterly (trade) wind. If the wind swings round to west or (worst of all) southwest, unsettled weather follows. The central mountains catch up the clouds carried by these winds; read the signs to find the best 'microweather' for your walk:

- **Strong winds** from any direction except east, bring rain, if not storms. (Eg, if a strong northeasterly blows in, we head for the southwest.)
- **Strong wind from the east or south of east** *(leste):* This hot, dry wind from Africa should make for good walking everywhere.
- **Mild winds from any direction except south or southwest** afford good walking all round the island, although the northern valleys may be cloudy.
- **Mild winds from the south/southwest** bring rain!
- As a rule of thumb, the **Desertas Islands** can serve as a 'ready-reckoner' for weather signs:
— If they are clearly visible (wind from W of N): the southeast, northeast and east are clear — at least in the valleys. The west is cloudy.
— If they are hazy or hardly visible (wind from the E, S, SE): the south may be cloudy, but walking is generally good everywhere.
— If they are cloudy (wind from the NE): the west, southwest and northwest are clear; eastern areas may be cloudy.
— If they seem very close and there is a white line on the horizon (wind from S, SW): rain is coming within 24 hours.

- The old adage invariably holds true: 'red sky at night, walkers' delight; red sky in the morning, take warning!'
- Telephone 12 150 for a recorded weather forecast *in Portuguese,* or see the inside back page of local newspapers.
- The general pattern is a clear morning, with clouds gathering by mid-day, and the sky clearing again by mid-afternoon. *Early starts are recommended!*

What to take

If you are already on Madeira and haven't walking boots or a torch or rucksack, you can still do many of our walks. But don't attempt the more difficult ones without proper equipment. For each walk in this book, we tell you the *minimum* equipment necessary. Where we require walking boots, there is *no substitute:* you will need to rely on the grip and ankle support they provide, as well as their waterproof qualities. For all other walks wear stout lace-up shoes with thick rubber or 'Vibram'-type soles, to provide good grip. Do *not* venture on walks requiring a torch unless you have one — some levada tunnels are exceedingly long, and you *must* be able to see both the roof (for possible projections) and the path, because the water in the channel may be very deep, cold, and fast-moving.

You may find the checklist below useful:

walking boots (which must be broken-in and comfortable)	windproof (zip opening)
	knives and openers
waterproof rain gear (outside summer months)	fleece
	bus timetables (see page 9)
water, water purifying tablets	sunhat, suncream, sunglasses
mobile phone	plastic rainhat
torch (with a wide beam)	extra pair of socks and bootlaces
telescopic walking pole(s)	'Dog Dazer' (see 'Nuisances')
long-sleeved shirt (sun protection)	plastic groundsheet
long trousers, tight at the ankles	plastic plates, cups, etc
first-aid kit, including bandages	whistle, compass

Please bear in mind that we've not done *every* walk in this book under *all* weather conditions: we may not realise just how hot — or wet — some walks might be. Walking boots are *always* more useful than shoes, and we wear them all year round. In hot weather, *always* carry a long-sleeved shirt as well as your sunhat, and take your lunch in a shady spot. We rely on your good judgement to modify our equipment lists according to the season.

Nuisances

Dogs are not often a problem, but a 'Dog Dazer' (ultrasonic dog deterrent) is a good investment. For details log on to www.sunflowerbooks.co.uk. There are *no* snakes, scorpions, poisonous spiders, or any other 'nasties' on the island.

Large **groups of walkers**, whether travelling by coach or in fleets of mini-buses or 4WDs, may cause your heart to sink, and they seem to invariably stop for lunch at the places recommended in this book. If you know they are on your path, it may be best to stop somewhere else to picnic.

Road-building over the life of this edition will sometimes interrupt walking routes for a short time (but we do not expect any of our walks to be affected in the long term). The new

Wait till your knees are used to Madeira's terrain before tackling steep descents like the path to Ilha (left, Walk 28) or the old ice-runners' path down the Levada da Negra (right, Walk 2)

roads *do* have advantages. They've opened up the mountains to less mobile tourists and are even speeding walkers who hire cars to their chosen paths! They have also enabled the local buses to extend their routes closer to some walks.

Portuguese for walkers

Once you venture off the beaten track, few of the older people speak English (the children often speak English or French). We have found an almost foolproof way to ask *and understand* directions in Portuguese. First, memorise the key questions and all their possible answers below; then **always phrase your questions so that you will get a yes ('seng') or no ('nowg') answer.**

KEY QUESTIONS (English/approximate Portuguese pronunciation)

'Please, sir (madam). **Fahz** fah-**vohr**, sehn-**yohr** (sehn-**yoh**-rah).

Where is the levada to ... **Ohn**-deh eh al leh-**vah**-dah **pah**-rah ...
  (the main road to ..., (ah ish-**trah**-dah **pah**-rah ...,
  the footpath to ..., ah veh-**ray**-dah **pah**-rah ...,
  the way to ..., oh cah-**mee**-noo **pah**-rah ...,
  the bus stop)? ah pah-**rah**-jeng)?
Many thanks.' **Mween**-too o-bree-**gah**-doo (a woman says: '**Mween**-too o-bree-**gah**-dah).

POSSIBLE ANSWERS (English/approximate Portuguese pronunciation)
here/there ah-**key**/ah-**lie**
straight ahead/behind **semp**-reh eng **frengt**/ah-**traash**
to the right/to the left ah deh-**ray**-tah/ah ish-**kehr**-dah
above/below eng **see**-mah/eng **bye**-joo

Ask a native speaker (your hotel porter, tour rep, or taxi driver) to help you with the pronunciation of these key phrases, as well as *place names*.

When you have your mini-speech memorised, always ask the many questions you can concoct from it in such a way that a yes/no answer will result. *Never* ask an open-ended question such as 'Where is the main road?' Even if you are standing on it, you probably won't understand the answer! Instead, ask the question and then **suggest the most likely answer yourself**, for example:

'**Fahz** fah-**voor**, sehn-**yoo**-rah. **Ohn**-deh eh ah ish-**tra**-dah **pah**-rah Foon-

shal? Eh **sem**-preh eng **frengt**?' or '**Fahz** fa-**vohr**, sehn-**yor**. **Ohn**-deh eh ah Le-**vah**-dah dosh **Tor**-nosh? Eh eng **see**-mah ah deh-**ray**-tah?'

An inexpensive phrase book will help you compose other 'key' phrases and answers. It is always pleasant to greet people you meet on your walks with a 'good morning' or 'good afternoon' (bohm **dee**-ah, bo-ah **tard**).

Organisation of the walks

Our walks are grouped in three general areas: the southeast; the northeast and the great peaks; the west and northwest. We urge you to walk in *each* of these three areas, in order best to sample the island's varied landscapes.

We hope that the book is set out so that you can plan your walks easily — depending on how far you want to go, your abilities and equipment, the season ... and what time you are willing to get up in the morning!

You might begin by looking at the fold-out touring map inside the back cover. Here you can see at a glance the overall terrain, the extent of the levada network, main and secondary roads, and the orientation of the walking maps in the text. Flipping through the book, you'll see that there is at least one photograph for each walk.

Having selected one or two potential excursions from the map and the photographs, turn to the relevant walk. At the top of the page you will find planning information: distance/time, grade, equipment, and how to get there. If the grade and equipment specifications are beyond your scope, don't despair! *We almost always suggest a short version of each walk* and, in most cases, these shorter walks are far less demanding of agility and equipment.

When you are on your walk, you will find that the text begins with an introduction to the overall landscape and then quickly turns to a detailed description of the route itself. Times are given for reaching certain key checkpoints. *Do compare your pace with ours on one or two short walks before tackling a long hike!* **Note that our times do not include any stops!** Allow extra time for picnics, photography, and any other breaks. Below is a key to the **symbols** on the walking maps.

▬▬▬	expressway	●▸	waterfall, tank, tap	⛪	church.chapel
▬▬▬	main road	*P*	picnic suggestion (see pages 12-16)	⊞	cemetery
———	minor road			†	shrine, statue
———	track	👓	best views		picnic site with
− − − −	footpath, cobbled trail	⁝	danger! vertigo!	⋒	tables
3 → ▭▭▭▭	main walk	🚌	bus stop	⊞	map continuation
3 → ⋯⋯⋯	alternative walk	🚗	car parking	⚡	relay station
———	levada, pipe	■	specified building		power station
2 → ———	levada walk	] [	tunnel	⚘	radio/TV mast
		—600—	altitude (metres)		bar/shop, café

APPETIZER: FROM SANTA TO PORTO MONIZ

See photograph page 32   **Distance:** 3km/2mi; 1h15min

Grade: moderate; a steep descent of 450m/1475ft. You must be sure-footed, but there is no danger of vertigo. *Virtually no shade*

Equipment: stout shoes (walking boots preferable), sunhat, optional picnic, water, walking stick, bathing things

How to get there: 🚌 80 or 139 to Santa; or 🚗: park by the public WC, 100m northeast of the church.

To return: 🚌 80 from Porto Moniz, back to base, or back to your car at Santa

While road-building has ruined many of Madeira's old trails, several relatively short stretches still remain and have even been restored. Walks 15, 18, 27b and 40, and Alternative walk 25-1 all include sections of old cobbled trails. This 'Appetizer' is the perfect way to stretch your legs on a car or bus tour to the northwest. The best way to do it is to drive or take a bus to Santa in the morning, walk slowly down, savouring the views, then have lunch and a swim at the sea-water pools in Porto Moniz, before catching the 4pm bus — back to base, or back to your car.

Start out on the main road in **Santa**, 100m northeast of the church: walk down the road signposted 'CAMINHO DO PICO'. Go straight over a crossroads (**5min**) and, when the tar ends, continue down a *very steep* concrete lane, already enjoying superb views over Porto Moniz and the large sea-water pool complex. When the concrete lane ends (**20min**), take concrete steps off right: these quickly give way to the old zigzag trail — much easier on the knees. The trail eventually runs into a valley — a pleasant shady interlude, before descending near the ER101. It's worth taking the pretty cobbled path back to the right, up to the most southerly of the hairpin bends in the road … to make the walk last longer!

When you pass near the restaurant/viewpoint on the right (on the next hairpin bend), keep left downhill. Five minutes later cross straight over a strip of concrete by some houses, on a narrower, steeper cobbled trail. Concrete steps take you down to a narrow levada not far above the school in **Porto Moniz**. Follow the levada to the right, then descend by road and steps (with street lights) to the POOL COMPLEX (**1h15min**). The bus leaves from the roundabout just above the pools.

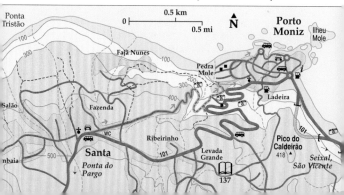

1 THE SOCORRIDOS VALLEY

Distance: 8.5km/5.3mi; 3h20min   **See also photograph page 7**

Notes: There is now a rock-crushing plant in the lower Socorridos Valley, which can be noisy. Try to save this walk for a Sunday. It is also possible to begin the walk at Barreiros Stadium (*town* 🚌 45; see plan pages 10-11), but the area surrounding the levada is very built-up.

Grade: moderate, with an ascent of 150m/500ft up to the Levada do Curral. You must be sure-footed and agile. **Possibility of vertigo**, but railings protect most of the exposed sections.

Equipment: stout shoes, sunhat, long-sleeved shirt, picnic, water

How to get there: *town* 🚌 2 to Quebradas
To return: *town* 🚌 8 or 16 from Madeira Shopping

Alternative walk: Levada do Curral. 7.5km/4.7mi; 2h. Grade and equipment as main walk (but there is no ascent). Take *town* 🚌 8 or 16 to Madeira Shopping. Walk downhill past the tower advertising Burger King on your left, and turn right immediately past the 'CEMA' building. After 100m/yds you can join the double-channelled Levada do Curral, which runs beside the road, on your right. (There are some narrow stretches here, as it rounds a tiny valley.) In 10min the narrow lane up from Pinheiro das Voltas comes in from the left, just before house 121. Now follow the main walk from the 1h28min-point to the end.

The magnificent Socorridos is the focal point for this walk. Just behind the noisy 'Ruhr Valley' river mouth, we are drawn into a magnificent tapestry of cultivation … which eventually unravels at a spectacular gorge.

Start at **Quebradas** (terminus for town bus 2). Walk straight ahead (west), past a supermarket, a turn-off to the expressway and the school (all on your left). Some 30m/yds past the school, opposite a tiled tap, cross the road and join the **Levada dos Piornais** (covered with concrete slabs). As you begin to round a small valley, the Socorridos bridge can be seen ahead. In **35min** you come to an information panel about the Piornais Levada, opposite a road left to Lombada.

Now the levada turns north. The ground falls away, and you edge the breathtaking **Ribeira dos Socorridos**. Within the next 10 minutes, take a break by a grassy verge, to admire the 'winged' bridge and the valley's tapestry of terracing. Sugar cane still persists along the muddy flats below in the river bed, and it's easy to imagine how nuns from the Santa Clara Convent fled to Curral under cover of cane in 1566.

Continuing along the levada, you will probably marvel at the golden curves of this watercourse hewn in the side of the rock … sheer sculpture. Now you approach a series of short tunnels (no torch needed). Although the path through them is well protected, some people will find this stretch vertiginous. If you *do* go through the tunnels, ***you will have to stoop down very low, so take off your rucksack, or it will catch on the roof.*** Otherwise, just follow the painted green arrow and descend steps to a path below the tunnels.

Whichever route you choose, you will come to crossing

Levada do Curral near the isolated house (2h15min)

concrete steps, where you turn right uphill. When the steps stop (10 minutes above the levada, by a house and a sign 'Vereda do Pico da Lombada' on the left), turn right on a cinder path, following street lights. Join a road at a T-junction and continue left uphill. In under 15 minutes from the top of the steps (**1h20min**) you reach a junction at **Pinheiro das Voltas**. Turn *left* here, climbing a lane, the TRAVESSA DO PINHEIRO DAS VOLTAS. The lane narrows. In eight minutes you reach the **Levada do Curral** at a T-junction with a road. Turn left here, passing house No 121 on the left. Now follow the levada past some pretty houses and gardens. After a brief diversion into the shady head of the **Ribeira do Arvoredo**, you soon find yourself once again at the edge of the Socorridos.

When the houses end (**1h55min**), you will come to a red warning sign (see page 36). But continue ahead; railings provide psychological comfort, and the route is not dangerous at this point. In under **2h15min** some well-tended vines spring up by a pretty, isolated house. Ignore a path down to the left through the vegetable plots 80 paces beyond it.* About 400m/yds past the house you will come to a gate. Unless there has been a landslide ahead, the gate should be open. But we suggest you *go only as far as the first unprotected drops on the left.* From this point you can see a sheer escarpment ahead, usually pouring with water and a jungle of vegetation. You have entered the gorge of the **Ribeira da Lapa** and will no doubt be as astonished as we were to find such an awesome place so close to Funchal. Ahead of you the aptly named hamlet of Fajã ('landslip') sits abandoned on a hillside. Below you the Ribeira da Lapa flows into the Ribeira do Curral and the two become the Socorridos. When you consider that these rivers cut the valley and today feed four *major* levadas, you can perhaps imagine what a torrent the Socorridos was when some of Zarco's men very nearly drowned in it (the word *socorridos* means 'rescued men').

Now turn back and *keep on the levada* past house 121, then make your way to MADEIRA SHOPPING (**3h20min**) — far nicer than its 'Burger King' tower would suggest! The BUS SHELTER shown on our map is where buses 8 and 16 stop.

*Experienced walkers could take this *very steep and slippery* path down to the confluence of the Lapa and Curral (allow 45min return and keep left at a fork partway down). Once down in the chasm, the source of the lower levada on the western side of the Socorridos lies not far to the left; the source of the Levada dos Piornais is just north of the Ribeira da Lapa.

2 FROM THE POÇO DA NEVE TO BARREIRA

Map begins on the reverse of the touring map and ends on page 43;
photographs pages 6, 13 and 39 (right)

Distance: 7.5km/4.7mi; 3h15min

Grade: moderate-strenuous; a steep descent of 900m/2350ft. You must
be sure-footed and have a head for heights (**danger of vertigo**).

Equipment: stout shoes (walking boots preferable), sunhat, picnic,
water; fleece, long trousers and windproof in cool weather

How to get there: 🚖 taxi to the Poço da Neve (ice house) on the ER202
2km below Pico do Arieiro, or 🚌 103 or 138 to Poiso (add 5km/3mi;
1h30min). The ice house is *below* the road, behind a walled lay-by.
To return: shuttle 🚐 91 from Barreira to Trapiche, then connecting *town*
🚐 10A or 11

Shorter walk: Poço da Neve — sheep pens — Poço da Neve. 4.5km/
2.8mi; 2h40min. Moderate; no danger of vertigo. Stout shoes, sunhat.
Access/ return: 🚖 car or taxi to/from the Poço da Neve. Follow the main
walk for 1h08min, then return the same way.

Alternative walk: Short walk 19 — Poço da Neve — Barreira. 11km/
6.8mi; 4h45min. 🚖 taxi to Pico do Arieiro. Grade, equipment, return
as main walk. Follow Short walk 19 (page 89) to the second viewpoint,
then walk down the ER202 to the ice house to start this walk.

This thoroughly exhilarating walk has it all: glistening
moorlands, a ribboning levada, and tremendous views.
But wait till you've acquired your 'Madeira knees' — it's
steep! So steep that it's unlikely any of the ice had a chance
to melt back in the early 1900s, when men shouldering the
precious commodity (wrapped in straw and packed in leather
bags) fairly *ran* from the *poços da neve* ('snow pits') below
Arieiro down to Funchal. The ice was not just served up in
sorbets and drinks to the sybarites, it had important medical
uses — to staunch bleeding, for example. Today only one
ice house has been preserved and only one of the descent
paths down into Funchal remains — the route we take down
the Santo António Valley.

Start out at the domed ICE HOUSE (**P**2) high on the eastern
flanks of the **Ribeira de Santa Luzia**. Your route begins on
the *western* side of the valley, where you can see a few paths
running along the ridge. The easiest way to get there is to
head *slightly left downhill* to the grove of squat heath trees
shown at the left in the photograph on page 13. *Ignore* the
track crossed a minute down, and *ignore* any signposts for
'Levada do Barreiro'. (The Barreiro route follows a levada on
the *eastern* side of the Santa Luzia Valley down to the Montado do Barreiro forestry house mentioned in the footnote on
page 26. When we tried this path years ago it was horrendous.
It has recently been repaired and waymarked, but is still
classified as 'difficult' and best done in a guided group.)

Once in the trees, you meet another crossing track. Turn
right here and head *back up* the valley. In **30min** you
encounter fencing: a gate, and then a stile, lead you to the

point where you must cross the ravine — just above one of the concrete walls built into the river bed to calm the rush of water after heavy rain and prevent further erosion. On the far side of the river bed, turn left and, about 15m/yds from the dam, watch for rocks on the right indicating the start of a clear earthen path. Follow this path up to a pass (**40min**), where you head right for about 10m/yds, to join the very narrow **Levada da Negra** (you cannot see the levada until you are almost upon it — be still for a moment and listen for the sound of its rushing water).

Turn left and let the levada guide you towards Funchal down a new valley — the **Ribeira de Santo António**. The city reveals itself in the V of the river valley. A rocky moonscape, with gnarled white heath tree limbs, alternates with ferny glens. Where the grassy pastureland is broken, luscious gold and russet volcanic hues emanate from the rock. On rounding a bend (**50min**), a picturesque spread of circular rock-built sheep pens appears on the right, stretching along a small plateau. Ten minutes later you can fork right across a shallow gully to visit the pens (**1h08min**), the setting for an annual shearing festival on 10th June.

Return to the levada. (*The Shorter walk heads back here.*) At **1h25min** you cross to the western side of the river. From now on the path is more eroded, and there are some vertiginous passages as the wild valley opens up below on the left. You'll have to be nimble, too, to negotiate a couple of awkward gullies. By **2h25min**, after you have passed below the trig point marking the summit of **Estéios**, there is a superb view down to the twin spires of Santo António's church; the single slender spire of São Martinho is silhouetted against the sea. Looking back up the valley, you can trace your route almost back to the sheep pens.

In just **2h35min** you pass through a gate and the steep descent ends, as you contour beneath a canopy of dense eucalyptus trees. In **2h40min**, two levadas shoot down to the left by a tiny waterhouse. Cross them and keep straight on, along this narrow and slippery red clay path. In **3h** you begin a new descent: turn left down a cobbled trail, with a rushing levada on either side. Soon enjoy another superb view — stretching from Boa Nova in the east to Cabo Girão in the west. Beyond a couple of isolated houses and a water tank on the left (**3h10min**), concrete comes underfoot. Three minutes later, at a Y-fork, keep *left* (the concrete lane ahead descends to Chamorra). In two minutes (**3h15min**) you reach **Barreira** — just a tarred turning circle for SHUTTLE BUS 91.

3 FROM THE EIRA DO SERRADO TO CURRAL

Map on reverse of the touring map   **Distance:** 3km/2mi; 1h30min

Grade: moderate descent of 450m/1475ft. In autumn and winter fallen chestnut leaves obscure the path, so watch your footing.

Equipment: stout shoes or walking boots, sunhat, water, optional picnic

How to get there: 🚗 to the Eira do Serrado viewpoint (Car tour 3) or 🚌 81 to the Eira turn-off on the ER107 (add 10min walking)

To return: 🚌 81 from the Curral road or Curral village — back to Funchal, or to the Eira turn-off, to collect your car (add 10min walking)

Alternative walk: Eira do Serrado — Levada do Curral. Approximately 6.5km/4mi; 3h35min. Grade as main walk, but **danger of vertigo.** Access/return, equipment as main walk. Do the main walk, then turn left on the road. The Levada do Curral is just over 15 minutes downhill, on the left, opposite a bus stop. There is a red warning sign here, indicating *very dangerous* (see page 36). The path is only 12 inches wide at best, with sheer drops almost immediately. It used to be possible to walk this exceedingly beautiful levada all the way to Funchal (linking up with the second half of Walk 1), but **we no longer recommend it even for experts.** Those with a very good head for heights should be able to follow it for about an hour. Then return the same way to the bus stop.

Until the 1950s the post (with vital funds sent home by emigrants) was carried from Funchal to Curral by a woman. Climbing and descending via the Eira, with her precious deliveries balanced in a basket on her head, she counted 52 hairpin bends each way. We follow the easiest part of her daily round.

Start out at the **Eira do Serrado**. First climb the aloe-fringed path at the left of the beautifully situated hotel; it leads to the famous viewpoint. Then return and descend the steps at the right of the sign 'EIRA DO SERRADO ALT. 1094 m' (**15min**). The steps lead into a beautiful old cobbled trail below chestnut trees. You clear the trees five minutes down, to be greeted by superb views (*P3*) — and you won't have to share

View to Curral das Freiras, near the end of the descent

them. As the trail makes a V-turn to the left, you are just level with the entrance to the old road tunnel under the Eira. On the far side of the Ribeira do Curral, the houses of Casas Próximas teeter on the *lombo* plunging off Pico do Serradinho.

As you descend close by the old road, you'll be a source of some amusement to passing motorists. S-bends take you past a couple of well-placed promontories; one of them (with an electricity pylon; **45min**) is a particularly pleasant picnic spot. From here there is a view back left to the first part of Walk 4: trees mark the Boca da Corrida, and the gorse-filled 'dip' between Pico Grande (with the twin summits) and Pico do Serradinho (to the left) is Boca do Cerro.

Beyond this promontory the sometimes-narrow path continues to drop sharply in more S-bends. In summer the surrounding cliffs are bright with yellow-flowering house-leeks. Soon you're just opposite Curral's church, in the setting shown on the previous page. When the road is not far below you, notice that the path *climbs;* don't try to scramble down too soon. Once on the ROAD (**1h15min**), you could turn left downhill to the nearest BUS STOP (5min) or descend to the levada (Alternative walk). Otherwise, walk 800m uphill to **Curral** (15min) — to the Vale das Freiras restaurant (on the right), for some unforgettable chestnut soup or cake!

Walk 4: the massive escarpment of Pico Grande, seen ahead, will rise 300m/1000ft sheer above us beyond the Boca do Cerro.

4 BOCA DA CORRIDA • PICO GRANDE • ENCUMEADA

Map on reverse of the touring map; photograph opposite

Distance: 13km/8mi; 4h

Grade: moderate ups and downs, with an overall climb of about 300m/ 1000ft and descent of 500m/1650ft; you must be sure-footed. Below the escarpment of Pico Grande the path is narrow (**possibility of vertigo**), often wet, and **sometimes impassable**, due to landslides.

Equipment: walking boots, long trousers, sunhat, picnic, plastic bottle/ water purifying tablets, whistle; extra fleece, windproof in cool weather

How to get there: 🚌 any of the many buses to Estreito de Câmara de Lobos; then taxi to Boca da Corrida. For those loath to spend the (fairly high) taxi fare: 🚌 96 to Jardim da Serra, from where it is a *very steep climb of about 350m/1150ft to Boca da Corrida*.
To return: 🚌 6 from Encumeada

Alternative walk: Boca da Corrida — Boca do Cerro — Corticeiras. 11.5km/7mi; 3h30min. Fairly easy. Stout shoes, sunhat, picnic, water. Access as for main walk; return on 🚌 96. Follow the main walk to Boca do Cerro; then return to Boca da Corrida and walk down the road from the forestry house. Just 1km beyond the hotel at Jardim da Serra, at a junction with signposting to 'Foro' and 'Jardim da Serra' (map pages 54-55), turn left uphill for 400m/yds, to the Pastelaria Santiago in Corticeiras, where the 96 'Corticeiras' bus stops. Or 🚗 to/from Boca da Corrida *(limited parking);* this shortens the walk by 4.5km/1h10min.

I f we had to choose our favourite mountain walk on the island, it would probably be this one. There is so much to recommend it: not only are the views magnificent throughout, but there's very little climbing! The first part of the walk, to the Boca do Cerro, is still fairly easy, despite the fact that the once-grassy trail has been badly eroded by groups of walkers in recent years. Rounding Pico Grande can sometimes be tricky, but most of the time the path is safe, and few people will find it vertiginous.

At the pass of **Boca da Corrida** there is a forestry house, a shrine, and a spectacular viewpoint over Curral das Freiras to the high peaks. As you face north, looking to the right of the shrine, Pico Grande rises ahead of you, framed in the V between Pico do Cavalo to the left and Pico do Serradinho to the right. Pico Grande is John's favourite mountain and easily identified from all over the island because of the rocky knoll on its summit. You'll see a path on the hillside to the left, but this is *not* our path. Out route is higher up and, for the moment, hidden from view; it runs just above the layer of broom, at the foot of the rock face with fencing.

Begin the walk by taking the stone-laid trail at the left of the SHRINE. In 30m/yds turn right (ignore the concreted track on the left between pillars; it is the route followed by Alternative walk 5 from the Casas do Dr Alberto). Then fork left on a stony path marked with an orange rectangle and a star (see page 36). (The path to the right goes to another

49

viewpoint.) You climb a rough trail, eventually passing to the right of the fencing you spotted from the pass. After **8min** the walk levels out and, from a promontory on the right, there are fine views of the high mountains towering above Curral.

The Vinháticos *pousada* and the Paúl da Serra come into focus from the **Boca dos Corgos**, a pass reached in **30min**. (Be sure to ignore the old trail down sharp left to Serra de Água here.) Beyond the **Passo de Ares** (**45min**), the path makes a wide arc along the flanks of **Pico do Serradinho**. By **1h10min** you reach the fourth pass, the **Boca do Cerro**. *(The Alternative walk turns back here.)* Beyond the Boca do Cerro, our route (which was the main north/south trail over the island in the 1800s) narrows appreciably, but it is easily discernible. Turn down left* through the prickly gorse (sign with an orange rectangle and three stars) and soon begin to skirt the awe-inspiring escarpment of **Pico Grande**. It will take 20-25 minutes to pass this rock face, where the *path is very narrow, often wet, and prone to landslides and forest fires*. Then the undulating path begins its descent towards Encumeada.

Beyond another escarpment, the **Fenda do Ferreiro**, you reach a sunny promontory above the knolls of **Piquinhos** (**2h05min**), with more fine views towards the Paúl da Serra. You pass a path down sharp left and, three minutes later, a spring on the right (**2h20min**). Soon you come into the enchanting valley of the **Ribeira do Poço**, emerald green and dotted with *palheiros* on grassy abandoned terraces. The main river is crossed on a grass-covered stone bridge (**2h 35min**). A still-cultivated *poio* pops up at the end of the valley (**3h05min**), followed by a promontory on the left overlooking the Pousada dos Vinháticos. Ignore a path down left to Serra de Água (**3h15min**).

Contouring through eucalyptus woods (often fire-scarred), you pass under the pipe carrying water from the Norte and Rabaças levadas (Walk 32; **3h45min**) down to the power station at Serra de Água. The path widens to a track, the Residencial Encumeada comes into view, and you meet the ER228 (**4h**). Wait for the BUS here: flag it down! Or walk 1km down to the *residencial* (10min), for a drink or snack.

*The path to the right quickly reaches Chão da Relva, a grassy area with chestnut trees — a lovely picnic spot. From here experienced mountain walkers can climb to the summit of Pico Grande (1h30min return) or descend to Curral (3h). Note the warning sign (red rectangle with three stars). The Pico Grande path forks left off the Curral path after a few metres/yards, to climb the eastern flanks of the mountain; it is easily seen and marked with cairns and intermittent paint spots. The two most exposed points (close to the bottom and again at the very top) are protected with fixed steel ropes. These routes are highlighted on the map with dashed green lines.

5 FONTES • ACHADA DA PINTA • TROMPICA • FONTES

Map on reverse of touring map; continuation pages 54-55

Distance: 11km/6.8mi; 3h35min

Grade: moderate climb and descent of 500m/1650ft on track. The initial ascent is tiring in hot weather.

Equipment: stout shoes (walking boots preferable), sunhat, picnic, water; extra fleece and windproof in cool weather

How to get there and return: 🚌 to Fontes, above Boa Morte. Travelling on the ER229, the road is 3km west of Campanário and 2.5km east of Ribeira Brava; it is signposted 'S João, S Paulo, Levada do Norte'. Beyond Boa Morte, cross the Levada do Norte in the pine forest (3.5km from the ER229), then continue north. Round the deep valley of the Ribeira Funda, ignore the turning left for Espigão, and drive past the impressive steps to São Paulo's church. Fontes is the next village, 1.4km north. Leave your car parked well off the road, so that the bus or any heavy lorry can turn round. Fontes is also accessible by 🚌 127 *from Ribeira Brava.*

Alternative walk: Fontes — Achada da Pinta — Trompica — Boca da Corrida — Corticeiras. 15.5km/9.6mi; 5h40min. *A more attractive return route than the track used in the main walk and especially recommended for those travelling by bus.* Moderate, but you must be sure-footed on the path in the Ribeira do Campanário. Equipment as above, but walking boots and long trousers recommended. Access by 🚌 127 or taxi; return on 🚌 96 from Corticeiras. At the Trompica forestry house (2h50min), climb up the earthen bank at the left of the track, to find a good but narrow path which circles the Ribeira do Campanário. If you come to any forks, be prepared to spend a few minutes searching out the correct, well-trodden path (it may be overgrown, depending on the season) and remember not to lose height. Some 20min from Trompica you'll be at the centre of the valley, with a photogenic cultivated knoll below you. Soon there is a delightful grove above the path, on the left. Two river tributaries, with lovely rock pools, are crossed on stepping stones and, in 40min, you reach the lowest of the 'Casas do Dr Alberto' (you will have spotted the three buildings on the property on your approach). Climb straight ahead here, at the left-hand side of this lowest stone shed. You come to the highest building, where you meet a track. Turn right on this track for Boca da Corrida. Another track comes in from above you, on your left, in about 1h10min, and you reach the forestry house at Boca da Corrida 1h40min from Trompica (4h30min). From here walk down the road from the forestry

Casa do Dr Alberto (Alternative walk)

house. Just 1km beyond the hotel at Jardim da Serra, at a junction sign-posted to 'Foro' and 'Jardim da Serra', you can catch a 96 'Foro' bus. Otherwise, turn left uphill for 400m/yds, to the Pastelaria Santiago in Corticeiras, where the 96 'Corticeiras' bus stops. *Special note: The path in the Campanário Valley is grazed by cows; we have often encountered up to a dozen on the narrow path. Be prepared to lose time here, shooing them away **quietly**. Approach the Casas do Dr Alberto quietly, too. Please protect the friendly welcome you will receive here for future walkers.*

Here's a walk that shows you the great divide formed by the Ribeira Brava from an unusual perspective. Not only will you have fantastic views over the north/south cleft of this deep ravine, but the panorama encompasses all the high peaks (Walks 19 and 20), Pico Grande (Walk 4), and the entire eastern escarpment of the Paúl da Serra. What's more, this is one of the few island walks that we can whole-heartedly recommend as a varied and satisfying circuit for those with hired cars.

At **Fontes** the asphalt road swings round to the right, but a concrete track rises at the right-hand side of the Bar Fontes (at the left of the 'Fontes' sign). **Start out** by climbing this track. It's a steep haul, especially tiring in hot weather, and there is *no shade*. But *don't* be discouraged by the dusty climb; once you reach the first pass, the way will become grassy and remain so for most of the walk.

The route takes you up the right-hand side of the **Ribeira Grande**. Within **35min** you will have crossed the **Ribeiro Frio** and be aiming for the first pass. On reaching it, the way becomes grassy. Look back to see the village of São Paulo. Small herds of cows will be encountered throughout the walk, grazing freely on this relatively level terrain.

Within **50min**, at another pass, you begin to enjoy the best views on the walk — the Ribeira Brava basin comes into

From fields of thistles and broom you look back down to São Paulo.

sight, as well as the Lombo do Mouro (Walk 31), Vinháticos, Pináculo (Walk 33), and Encumeada. As you round **Pico da Cruz** (**1h**), be sure to keep right (due south) on the track, where a path descends to the left. The grassy track takes you through fields of spring-blooming thistles, foxgloves and broom; a meadow lies below. In the past barley was grown up here (the reason for cutting the track), but it did not flourish. Yet another pass, reached in **1h10min**, opens up more views to the high peaks, from Grande round to Ruivo, via Pico do Gato and the Torres.

Beyond another pass, at about **1h25min**, you come to a Y-fork. The track to the right is the return route but, for the moment, go straight ahead. After some 25m/yds you may have to negotiate a makeshift stile in a fence. Some 15 minutes later (**1h40min**) you may encounter another fence with a similar stile. After another seven minutes the track makes a 90° turn to the left and ends at a pass (**1h50min**). Climb up half-right towards the summit. You will reach a small rock enclosure on the **Achada da Pinta** within seven minutes. At the far right-hand corner, stones have been placed to allow you to climb over carefully, without disturbing the wall. Inside the enclosure is a triangulation point, where a blue 'hat' is painted on the concrete — a fanatical Madeiran walker's way of saying 'Kilroy was here' (you will see these blue 'hats' on almost all your walks). From here you have a new outlook — over Curral's setting and even down to Funchal.

If you have time and the day is clear, it's worth spending some time up here to find your own favourite viewpoint! Then leave the triangulation point by climbing over the wall where you came in and retrace your steps to the fork first met in 1h25min (**2h25min**). Turn down sharp left. The track descends through a couple of gates and past minor tracks to the right and the left, which you ignore. By **2h45min** you're walking beneath sweet chestnuts and eucalyptus, but the track is no longer grassy. Five minutes later (**2h50min**) the **Trompica** forestry house is met, on your right. (*Here the Alternative walk leaves us, by taking the path up to the left of the track.*)

Continue down past the forestry house on the track. Allow 45 minutes for the tedious return to Fontes. Some 30 minutes below Trompica you come to a T-junction with an asphalt road.* Keep right here (left goes to Lugar da Serra and Campanário), descending at first, then climbing gently back to **Fontes**, 1km away (**3h35min**).

*A very short section of this road is not shown on our *walking* map; see the touring map or the walking map on pages 54-55.

6 LEVADA DO NORTE: FROM ESTREITO DE CÂMARA DE LOBOS TO BARREIRAS

Distance: 22km/13.6mi; 6h20min

Grade: easy, but long; a few sections demand a head for heights

Equipment: stout shoes, sunhat, picnic, water, torch; extra fleece and windproof in cool weather

How to get there: 🚌 96 to the levada crossing, 0.7km north of Estreito's church; ask for the 'Levada do Norte' bus stop.

To return: 🚌 6, 7, 80, 127 or 148 from Barreiras

Short walks

1 Estreito — Nogueira (1h40min) or Cabo Girão (2h30min). Easy, but some narrow stretches demand a head for heights. Equipment and access as main walk. Follow the main walk for 1h35min and catch a bus on the ER229. Or go on to Cabo Girão: continue on the levada to the tunnel (the 1h 55min-point) but, instead of curling right through it, keep ahead alongside a narrow levada. You will pass two steeply stepped paths down towards Câmara de Lobos. When you come to a road, follow it 500m/yds uphill to the right, to the viewpoint (about 35min from the tunnel). If no 🚌 154 is due, walk back down to the ER229.

2 Quinta Grande — Campanário. 8km/5mi; 2h. Grade and equipment as main walk. Access: 🚌 6, 7, 123, 139, 142 or 148 to 'Ribeira da Quinta Grande', where the ER229 crosses the levada. Follow the main walk from the 2h10min-point to the 3h45min-point, then descend to the ER229 at Campanário (frequent buses).

3 Boa Morte circuit. 4.5km/2.8mi; 1h20min. Easy; *highly recommended for beginners or those with hired cars*. Wear sensible shoes and take a picnic. Access/return: any 🚌 to Ribeira Brava, then 🚌 127 to Boa Morte. From Boa Morte follow the road uphill to the levada in the pine forest and turn left along it (*P*6), picking up the main walk at the 4h35min-point. Return to Boa Morte in time for 🚌 148. 🚗: Turn off the ER229 for 'S João, S Paulo, Levada do Norte' 3km west of Campanário. Drive through Boa Morte and park near the levada (3.5km *from the ER229*).

Alternative ending: The 2000 steps. *Sure-footed* walkers can end the main walk or Short walk 3 with a truly *spectacular* descent (walking stick recommended). Continue on the levada past the first lookout (5h), with more wonderful views over the valley. Ignore a path down left, cross a stream and, 25 minutes along, cross over a path with street lights. Some 12 minutes later, turn left on a road down to Eira do Mourão. Then descend concrete steps from the upper end of the small parking bay on your left, following street lights. Almost 2000 steep steps will take you down 500m/1650ft to Fajã on the ER104, where you could catch 🚌 6. Allow 1h30min for this descent (a total time of 7h for the main walk or 2h35min for Short walk 3). But if you have missed the bus, you will have to walk another 2km south into Ribeira Brava.

Allll year round this is a superb walk through a landscape rich in cultivation, thanks to the waters of the Levada do Norte (see notes in Walk 32). Here in early autumn the

grapes are harvested for some of Madeira's best-known wines; the valleys are thick with sugar cane and cherry trees.

When the bus roars up the hill at Estreito, you'll first pass the church and then a chapel on the left. Just round the next bend is the BUS STOP, called 'Levada (do Norte)'. **The walk starts** here, on the west side of the road, where you take a paved path under photogenic vine-bearing trellises. The levada is hidden under concrete at first. You'll hear it singing underfoot and soon reach the end of the covered walkway. Look left now, for good views of São Martinho Church and, on a clear day, the Desertas Islands.

At about **20min**, just as you bend right into the narrow **Ribeira da Caixa**, *watch for two separate paths down left, a few minutes apart, which avoid awkward, narrow ledges with overhanging rock.* Soon you'll find yourself deep in the valley; in May it is smothered in cherry blossoms. You cross a tributary and then the main river (**45min**) on levada bridges.

On leaving the valley, start counting churches to measure your progress. At **1h05min** here's the first, below at **Garachico** (see opposite). Five minutes later, climb steps to a road (where a 'Bar' is advertised up to the right); the levada is on the far side, 25m/yds downhill. At **Nogueira**, the levada seems to end at a brightly-painted house (**1h35min**). Descend the concrete ramp/steps on the left and, when you meet a cobbled road, climb it to regain the levada. *(But end Short walk 1 by turning left on the road, down to the ER229.)*

Staying on the levada, follow a stabilised path over a landslide (1999) caused by the factory which still looms up to the right. In six to seven minutes you cross the ER229. Drawing ever closer to Cabo Girão, enjoy the splendid views of the coast above **Caldeira**. Just before you curl right through the Cabo Girão tunnel at **Cruz da Caldeira** (**1h55min**), some

sheer drops are encountered, but they are protected by railings. (You may wish to take a detour here to Cabo Girão; see notes for Short walk 1 on page 54.) It only takes three minutes to walk through this tunnel and it *can* be managed without a torch, since the path is wide and the roof is high. Now Cabo Girão has disappeared, and you're in the **Ribeira da Quinta Grande**. At **2h10min** the levada skirts the

Boa Morte pine forest

The splendid vineyards below the church at Garachico

river bridge below the ER229. *Before you reach the parapet,* climb right up a dirt path to the main road. (*Short walk 2 begins here on the west side of the road,* where the levada is covered with concrete for a short distance; deduct 2h 10min from times below.)

At **2h25min** count the second church — at **Quinta Grande** — as you continue along another high and narrow stretch, parallel with the ER229. Soon come to a spot that's exceptionally lovely in the autumn: stately pillars of pine and sweet chestnut stand proud in iron-rich soil, and the forest is alive with pink belladonna lilies. Further on, the houses are festooned with dahlias and the aroma of wood fires is in the air. On roof-tops, marrows and beans almost strangle the charming chimneys.

Count the church of Campanário off to the west and start heading up the valley of the **Ribeira do Campanário**, golden with gorse and broom in spring. At about **3h10min** there are some very severe drops to the left, but they are secured by heavy iron railings. Soon you see the ER229 above Campanário — the square-shaped U-turn is very easily recognised. Cross the Ribeira do Campanário on a levada bridge in an ivy-creepered nook (**3h35min**).

Continue through the wooded heights above **Campanário** and in 10 minutes (**3h45min**) you'll cross a dirt track. (*If you are doing Short walk 2, leave here:* go straight down the track — do not take the left-hand fork. Descend to the ER229, where you'll find a bus stop and a bar/shop.)

Those continuing on the levada will cross a concrete lane beside a first waterhouse and then the tarred road to Lugar da Serra at **4h10min**. A football pitch is just below the levada, on the east side of the road. Eight minutes later pass a lovely little ruin on the right, with a grassy *poio* and chestnut trees — a delightful spot for a break. Soon you enjoy a fine view over the graceful arc of the expressway.

Just beyond a large waterhouse you meet the road down to Boa Morte (**4h35min**; *Short walk 3 comes in here*). Cross the road (the bar/café O Pinheiro is down to the left) and continue in the exceptionally beautiful setting shown opposite (***P**6*): the levada mirrors the trees, and the path is soft with pine needles. But this once-beautiful, large forest is slowly disappearing as trees are felled for housing.

Some 12-13 minutes after crossing the Boa Morte road, note a dirt track off left (**4h48min**). For the moment pass it by; soon you will have magnificent views north and south over the great cleft of the Ribeira Brava, its terraces, poplars, and banana plantations (**5h**; *P*6). This levada flows from far, far north of the viewpoint. (You could easily follow it to Eira do Mourão for the 'Alternative ending', or go as far as the first tunnel (1h), but the path will become extremely vertiginous, and there is no protective fencing. *Experts:* it's 13km/8mi; 4h30min of almost constant 'exposure' — or long tunnels! — from here to the power station at Serra de Água; a torch is essential.)

Return from your viewpoint to the track first passed at 4h48min and descend to **Boa Morte** (**5h40min**). It's unlikely you will catch the last bus of the day, so walk down to the ER229 at **Barreiras** (**6h20min**). The BUS SHELTER is opposite.

Eira do Mourão (Alternative descent) and the Ribeira Brava Valley

7 LEVADA DOS TORNOS: FROM ROMEIROS TO THE SÍTIO DAS QUATRO ESTRADAS

Distance: 27.5km/17mi; 7h30min (but see Short walks below).

Grade, equipment, how to get there and return: see Short walks.

Short walks: This walk breaks conveniently into the four stages described below. We begin at Romeiros, to avoid climbing to the levada. If you wish to begin at Monte or Babosas (a small square just east of the cable car terminus; access by *town* 🚌 20, 21, 22 or 🚠), follow the dashed green line on the map. The path to Romeiros leaves Babosas between the chapel shown on page 65 and the concrete seats at the viewpoint (various signs, including 'Levada dos Tornos'). *Important note:* 350m/ yds below Babosas, *there is a critical choice of paths. If you have a head for heights, keep left on the earthen path signposted 'Levada dos Tornos'. If you do not, curl downhill to the right on the main cobbled trail with street lights;* it will take you to Romeiros, where you can pick up Short walk 1 (page 60). The path to the left rises gently for just over 15 minutes, to join the levada at the point where it emerges from a long tunnel and rounds the upper João Gomes Valley — a truly primeval setting. While there *are* some protective railings, those prone to vertigo will find the going very tough!

1 Romeiros — Palheiro Ferreiro. 6km/3.7mi; 1h30min. Easy. Stout shoes, sunhat, picnic, water. *Town* 🚌 29 to Romeiros; return from the the levada crossing on the ER102 at Palheiro Ferreiro on 🚌 29 or 77 or *town* 🚌 37. (Or stop at one of the two tea houses en route and return on *town* 🚌 47.) If you end the walk with a visit to the Palheiro Gardens (open 09.30-16.30 Mon-Fri, except holidays), note that it also has a pleasant snack bar/restaurant, and you can return from there on *town* 🚌 36 or 37. Notes begin on page 60.

2 Palheiro Ferreiro — Camacha. 5.5km/3.4mi; 1h40min. Easy, but there is a very awkward tunnel (10 minutes) and a stiffish climb of 100m/330ft from Ribeirinha up to Camacha. Stout shoes (boots preferable), sunhat, picnic, water and a *good torch* for each member of the party. *Town* 🚌 37 or 🚌 29 or 77 to the ER102 at Palheiro Ferreiro; ask for 'Levada dos Tornos'. Return from Camacha on 🚌 29 or 77 (or from Nogueira on 🚌 110 or 114). Notes begin on page 61.

3 Camacha — Lombo Grande. 6km/3.7mi; 1h30min. Easy, but *you must be sure-footed, and there is a **danger of vertigo**:* the path is very narrow in places. Blackberry thorns sometimes intrude, and you may have to walk *through* (seasonal) waterfalls. Equipment as for Short walk 2 above, plus extra fleece, long trousers, windproof in cool weather, whistle. *Don't forget the torches!* 🚌 29 or 77 to Camacha; return from Lombo Grande on 🚌 60, or walk 1km uphill to Boqueirão for 🚌 110 or 1.6km uphill to Águas Mansas for 🚌 77. Notes begin on page 64.

4 Lombo Grande — Sítio das Quatro Estradas. 11.5km/7.1mi; 3h. Grade and equipment as Short walk 3, *but this stretch of levada is even more vertiginous* and there is a tiring climb of 150m/500ft to the Sítio das Quatro Estradas. Access: 🚌 60 (ask for 'Levada dos Tornos, Lombo Grande'). From the bus stop, walk north up the ER206 for one minute to the levada. Or take 🚌 77 to Águas Mansas or 🚌 110 to Boqueirão, then walk down to the levada (1.6km below Águas Mansas). Notes begin on page 64.

Alternative walks: By referring to the maps on pages 60-63, you can put together some interesting combinations with Walk 8, 9 or 10. You shouldn't have any difficulty, either, reversing Short walks 1, 2 or 3 (route-finding on Short walk 4, however, could be difficult in reverse).

The pull-out touring map gives you a good overview of the **Levada dos Tornos**. Inaugurated in 1966, it is Madeira's most important levada, with 106km (66mi) of main channels. Water collected from three chief sources in the north flows to the power station at Fajã da Nogueira. (You can explore the northern reaches of the Tornos on Walks 23 and 24.)

From the power station at Fajã da Nogueira (Walk 24) the levada flows through a very long tunnel (there are 16km/10mi of tunnels on the Tornos!) to the south of the island. It emerges into the open in the upper reaches of the João Gomes Valley, north of Romeiros, and then meanders on to irrigate more than 100,000 outlets between Funchal and Santa Cruz. And it is this southern run of the Tornos that we describe in the walk. From a height of 600m (almost 2000ft), the hustle and bustle of life at sea level seems very far away; walking this levada path is like overflying the south coast in a balloon.

Start Short walk 1 at the BUS TERMINUS in **Romeiros**. Climb steps and then the concrete path on the west side of the turning circle for the bus. Just where the concrete ends and cobbles begin, turn right, up concrete steps. (If you pass below a building with a flagpole, you have gone too far.) At the top of the steps, you are on the levada, but it is covered with concrete. Turn right on this covered walkway; you'll soon see the levada in full flow.

Follow the levada through groves of pine and mimosa, eventually passing through the grounds of the CHOUPANA RESORT HOTEL (**20min**). On meeting a crossing road (which leads south to the JARDIM BOTÂNICO; **35min**), walk a few metres downhill to the right, then go through the doorway

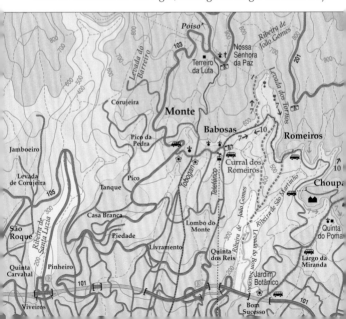

opposite (sign: LEVADA DOS TORNOS. A chapel is on your right; it belongs to the QUINTA DO POMAR, which you quickly pass.

In about **1h** you pass steps up left to a stop for town bus 47. Some 200m/yds further on, more steps lead up left to the HORTENSIA tea house, in beautifully landscaped gardens. Cross the ER201 (**1h10min**) and, three minutes later, pass above the JASMIN tea house. In **1h30min** you reach the ER102. Approach *carefully* — traffic roars round the blind bend to the left. *(Short walk 1 ends here; follow this busy road 200m/yds downhill to the right, to a bus shelter.* The PALHEIRO GARDENS are several minutes further downhill, on the left, almost opposite the ER201 to Terreiro da Luta — and another BUS STOP).

Short walk 2 begins at the **Levada dos Tornos** BUS STOP. The signposted levada is 100m/yds downhill from the stop. Head east in a delightful setting, bright with flowers and ochre-red soil. Almost at once you overlook **Palheiro Ferreiro**, the south coast, and the Desertas Islands. In three

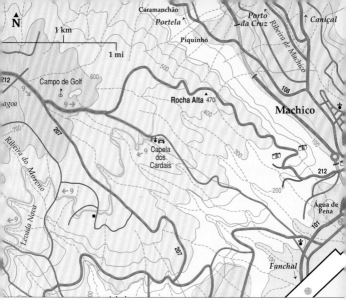

minutes you pass a school on your right. Walk to the left of another large building; a small stadium is above you, on the left. Cross a road and rejoin the levada by turning *sharp* left. Fragrant mimosa and eucalyptus grace the next stretch.

In **20min** you come to a tunnel. *Watch your head: the roof is low and jagged.* (The path to the right of the tunnel would take you uphill to a bar/shop, but you would have a very slippery descent back to the levada. This route is highlighted on the map with dashed green lines, but we recommend going through the tunnel.) You emerge 10 minutes later, soon coming to pleasant pine groves.

As you enter the valley of the **Ribeira do Caniço**, sprinkled with apple blossom in spring, look to the far side: you will see a road with street lights. When you come into the village of **Nogueira**, you must leave the levada: go left up concrete steps to join this road and follow it to the right uphill. There are fine views down right over Caniço. Once in the large housing estate, ignore all crossroads and keep ahead uphill. Pass a stop sign and walk ahead past the TERMINUS FOR BUS 114, to a T-junction with the ER205 (Caniço road; **1h05min**).

Turn left but, one minute uphill, at the boundary of the Laboratório Agricola, turn right. Go straight over a cross-roads, down into the village of **Ribeirinha** (BUS 111 STOP). Follow the road across a bridge* and up out of Ribeirinha,

---

*To continue on the levada, take the path by a large white arrow signpost 'Levada dos Tornos' (it *may* be hidden in greenery) on your right, 50-100m/yds past the bridge. At a first fork, ignore a path off to the right. (Over to the right are the ruins of a beautiful rose-painted house with a timbered balcony.) Five minutes off the road, at a Y-fork, bear right. You reach the levada in a minute: turn left. Pick up the notes for Short walk 3 at the 23min-point (the house with the magnifent palm).

to a T-junction. Go left uphill here, with glimpses down right over the Porto Novo Valley. Ignore a tarred road off to the right; keep left and rise steeply, to cross almost straight over the Camacha bypass. Passing a modern church on your right, you come into **Camacha** by the village square, the Achada da Camacha (**1h40min**), where the CAFÉ/ESTALAGEM DO RELÓGIO is on your right.

Start Short walk 3 facing the CAFÉ/ESTALAGEM DO RELÓGIO in **Camacha**'s square (Achada da Camacha). Descend the road at the right of the café (signposted to Funchal; a bank is on your right and a modern church left). Ignore a small road off right, cross the bypass road and continue down the road almost directly opposite (just a few metres to the right). In **7min** fork right and then look left for a fine view over the Porto Novo. A few minutes later, turn left at a T-junction. Watch for where the road crosses the **Levada dos Tornos** (by a small parking bay; **14min**) and turn left on the levada.

Having passed a house with a magnificent palm tree and a road on the right (**23min**)*, you come to a tunnel under the Salgados road a minute later. You'll need your torch, although it takes only three minutes to get through. Another tunnel is met in **40min** (two minutes; no torch needed). Beyond this tunnel there is a possibility of vertigo for, although the levada path is very adequate, there is no protective fencing, and the drops are severe — perhaps 50m/150ft. Often waterfalls cascade onto the path as well, and you may get soaked. Watch out, too, for the concrete blocks in the path, supporting the pipe carrying some of the water. Still, we hope you will manage this part of the walk in the lower part of the **Ribeira do Porto Novo** (see also Walk 8), because it is one of the most beautiful stretches of the Tornos. Suddenly birds and cascades are singing everywhere. In **50min** the levada makes a U-turn high in the valley, below some pools. The waterfall shown opposite crashes into the river; all else is stillness. This is an idyllic picnic spot.

Eight minutes from the pools you pass a dyke on the right and a *palheiro*. Pass through the third and shortest tunnel (**1h**), before skirting round a tunnel with 'windows' at about **1h10min** (be sure to climb up steps beyond this tunnel to rejoin the Tornos; the levada continuing ahead runs down to Gaula). This is another lovely picnic spot (*P*7a). Across the valley you can see Salgados, dribbling down the ridge (Walk 8). All too soon, you reach a reservoir at **Lombo Grande**. Beyond it is the ER206 (just over **1h30min**). Turn right and descend for under a minute to the BUS STOP.

Short walk 4 begins where the ER206 crosses the levada

*The road at the palm tree house first descends a bit, then rises to a T-junction, where a right turn leads to the 10min-point in Walk 8.

Along the Tornos (clockwise): old house at Nogueira, waterfall at the head of the Porto Novo Valley, flower-filled channel near Romeiros, rose-painted house at Ribeirinha (see footnote on page 63), statue at the Quinta do Pomar, and chapel at Babosas (alternative starting point).

at **Lombo Grande**. Head east; in under **10min** you have good views over the airport and São Lourenço Point. After **20min** you pass through a very short tunnel (no torch is needed, but it is very low: watch your head!) and come out in the **Ribeira da Boaventura** (**P**7b). While the Porto Novo is our favourite part of the Tornos in spring, in summer the Boaventura Valley (see page 66) takes the prize. The terraces are golden with wheat, and the levada paths are aglow with blue and white agapanthus — so tall and thick that they are almost like hedgerows. Most walkers will have no difficulty following the levada for a good 20 minutes past the tunnel, but then the way becomes vertiginous, as it delves into a very deep tributary, the **Ribeira dos Vinháticos**. By **50min** you reach the head of this stream. The next, smaller tributary, is a basin full of willow. In just over **1h35min** you pass a waterhouse on the left; beyond it is an asphalt road. Two minutes later a second asphalt road is crossed (**1h40min**). Both lead up to the ER102 at João Frino, if you're pressed for time and trying to catch bus 77. Beyond the second road you delve into the upper reaches of a new valley — the **Ribeira de Santa Cruz**. Ignore all the cobbled trails and paths crossing the levada during the next 45 minutes or so; civilisation seems very far away, as you enter an emerald wilderness.

Then suddenly, at **2h25min**, the levada ends. Unbelievable! How can this magnificent watercourse, which has carried you through the most beautiful valleys in the southeast, have abandoned you without warning? Its waters shoot out into a tank some 200m/650ft below, to feed the Levada

Picnic 7b, in the upper Boaventura Valley, looks out to these colourful terraces, spilling down a ridge between the Vinháticos and João Frino rivers.

Nova (see Walk 9). A pipe coming in from the Levada da Serra (Walk 10) runs down and over to the *lagoa* (reservoir) above Santo da Serra.

Walk back along the levada. In two minutes you pass a narrow path on the left (Walk 9 ascends it, from the Levada Nova; the descent is *not* recommended). Four minutes later, turn right up cobbled steps. A few minutes uphill, you emerge in fields. Head towards the electricity wires in front of you, keeping to the left of the plots. At a stone wall, bear left. Bear left again at a second wall, quickly coming to a cobbled track. Go left uphill (past the entrance to a *quinta*), to a crossroads. Here go straight ahead.* When a tarred road joins you from the left, continue straight ahead (right), climbing to the ER102 at the **Sítio das Quatro Estradas** (**3h**). Your BUS SHELTER is across the road.

*If you turn right here, you can follow a track to the church at Santo da Serra (see dashed green route on the map). You first skirt the grounds of the mysterious *quinta*, overgrown with luxuriant vegetation. For a short time in the 1800s it was home to a young Scottish doctor, Robert Reid Kalley, esteemed by the islanders for his near-miraculous cures. But he was also a Protestant, and when the authorities would no longer tolerate his incessant proselytising, he had to flee the island dressed as a woman. At a fork, be sure to keep right. Cross the Ribeira Serra de Água and rise through housing, where tar comes underfoot. Allow 30 minutes.

8 CAMACHA • LEVADA DO CANIÇO • ASSOMADA

Map pages 62-63; photo page 16   **Distance:** 6km/3.7mi; 2h20min

Grade: moderate, but with a very steep — sometimes slippery — descent of 250m/820ft to the levada. Surefootedness is essential; **possibility of vertigo** on the levada

Equipment: walking boots, long trousers, sunhat, picnic, water; extra fleece and windproof in cool weather

How to get there: 🚌 29 or 77 to Camacha
To return: 🚌 2 (or one of many others) from Assomada

Short walk: Assomada — Porto Novo Valley — Assomada. See notes for Picnic 9, page 13.

Alternative walk: Levada dos Tornos — Ribeirinha — Assomada. 11km/ 6.8mi; 3h40min. Grade and equipment as main walk; access as *Short walk 7-2, page 59.* Follow Short walk 7-2 (page 63), but do not climb into Camacha; keep on the levada at Ribeirinha (see the footnote on page 63). When you come to the house with the magnificent palm tree, refer to the footnote on page 64 to join this walk at the 10min-point.

Any season, any time of day, is suitable for this splendid walk in one of Madeira's most lush valleys. And this is a less vertiginous way to see the lower Porto Novo Valley than by following Walk 7; although the drops on this walk are quite severe, they are not as *sheer.*

Start out at the medical centre (CENTRO DE SAÚDE) in **Camacha**'s square (the Achada da Camacha): descend the steep tarred lane on the left-hand side of this building (sign-posted 'ASSOMADA, LEVADA DOS TORNOS, GAULA'), crossing over the bypass road. In **10min** ignore a turning right to the Levada dos Tornos. *(The Alternative walk joins here.)* Continue ahead to a fork at the school, then turn left. The tar quickly gives way to a lily-bordered cobbled path. It descends very steeply into the delightful 'perched' hamlet of **Salgados**, hidden in apple trees and decorated from top to toe with willow. Following electricity wires, keep on the same path. Pass a TAP on the right and, 10 minutes later, slither down stone 'steps', which drop you abruptly onto the **Levada do Caniço** (**35min**). Turn right to ramble to Assomada.

About 100m beyond a short tunnel, a particularly lovely promontory is met in **1h40min** (*P*8; see photograph page 16). Here you can picnic nestled in sugar cane, poppies and thistles — while you look out over the valley, the expressway bridge over the mouth of the river, and the Desertas Islands.

When the levada turns right, away from the valley, you'll see a large round water tank ahead on the left. Turn left down a concrete path just past this tank (just *before* a house; **2h**). A mill race raised up on pillars is on your left. You reach a road in half a minute. Turn left and follow the road downhill, past an electricity substation on your right. Walk behind the church at **Assomada** (**2h20min**) and, on meeting the ER204, turn left. The BUS STOP is on the east side of the church.

9 SANTO DA SERRA • LEVADA NOVA • SÍTIO DAS QUATRO ESTRADAS

Map pages 62-63   **Distance:** 14km/8.7mi; 4h

Grade: easy-moderate, with a steep climb of 250m/820ft at the end of the walk. You must be sure-footed and have a head for heights (**possibility of vertigo**). *Note:* This walk is best done between early May and October (see caption opposite). We also recommend that you do the walk in the direction described. Trying to descend to the levada from the Sítio das Quatro Estradas is difficult — the path is hard to find and, once you are on it, the descent is very steep and slippery.

Equipment: stout shoes (walking boots preferable), long trousers, sunhat, picnic, water; extra fleece and windproof in cool weather

How to get there: 🚌 20, 77 or 78 to Santo da Serra (or 🚗). If you object to a long walk on tarmac, take a taxi from there to the Capela dos Cardais, where the levada walk starts (deduct 40min).

To return: 🚌 77 from the Sítio das Quatro Estradas (or same bus or 🚗 from Santo da Serra; add 15min)

Short walk: Santo da Serra — Levada Nova — Sítio das Quatro Estradas (or Santo da Serra). 7km/4.3mi; 2h25min. Grade, equipment, access/ return as main walk. Follow the main walk for 6min, but at the Quinta da Paz fork right instead of left. Follow the tarred lane (later concreted) 3km down to the levada (keeping right at a fork 2.5km downhill), then pick up the main walk at the 2h20min-point. This option takes in the loveliest part of the walk.

If you've walked the Levada dos Tornos from start to finish, wouldn't you think that you'd seen the best of the Santa Cruz Valley? After all, the Tornos is 100m/330ft higher than the Levada Nova. Wouldn't you expect it to be greener, more vertiginous, more beautiful and more exciting than this lower levada? You are in for a surprise!

Start out at the CHURCH in **Santo da Serra**. Follow the ER212 southeast, past the park and a hotel on your left. At the Y-fork in front of the QUINTA DA PAZ (**6min**) bear left. *(But go right for the Short walk).* You pass the golf course on your left and the *lagoa* (reservoir) on the conical hill above right. Beyond the clubhouse for the golf course, you reach another fork. Go left towards 'Machico' and continue for about eight minutes, to another fork, where you go right towards 'Água de Pena'. Ten minutes' descent brings you the CAPELA DOS CARDAIS, on your right (**40min**). Climb the steps between the chapel and a large water tank to join the **Levada Nova**.

As you head west, the way is graced by *Senecio* and passion flowers, but some blackberry thorns tear at your long trousers too. You cross the ER207 running south to the airport at **1h18min**. Three minutes later, beyond a track, you come to a sizeable piggery. A couple of stone-laid trails cross your way not far beyond here.

Having rounded the **Ribeira do Moreno** and crossed a concrete road, in **2h20min** you meet another concrete road *(the Short walk rejoins here).* Cross the road; a waterhouse

Hidden in a glen of fuchsias are some pretty rock pools in the upper reaches of the Ribeira de Santa Cruz — a delightful spot to take a break, before heading back to Santo da Serra's highlands. The bridge is often washed away in storms and replaced by a ford, which may be impassable after heavy rains. Since the levada is also often blocked by fallen trees after high winds, this walk is best saved for the summer months!

is on your right. The levada is appreciably wider now, as you head up into the **Ribeira de Santa Cruz**. This stretch is guaranteed to delight even the most jaded levada-walker. Masses upon masses of blue and white agapanthus dance along the curves of the channel, a waterfall bursts upon the scene and then, in **2h55min**, you come to an emerald-green fern-covered grotto. But there is more to come: river pools shimmer down to the left, and soon you're in a glen of wild fuchsias. It's all too wonderful to last, and it doesn't. Almost at once the source of the levada is met at a water catchment, where overspill water pours in from the Levada dos Tornos above. A pipe (some of it underground) carries water here from the Levada da Serra (Walk 10) as well. Another pipe, this one visible, runs up to the *lagoa* above Santo da Serra.

From the water catchment, return to a path on your right, just over a minute along, and descend to a bridge or ford over the river, then climb the path on the far side *(turning sharp left some 3m/yds uphill)*. You struggle up to the **Levada dos Tornos** in 15 minutes. Turn right and follow it for two minutes, to where it ends and spills over into the water tank you've just left (**3h25min**). Turn back here and use the notes in the last paragraph on page 66, to climb to the **Sítio das Quatro Estradas** (**4h**), or see the footnote on the same page to go direct to Santo da Serra, if you've left your car there.

10 LEVADA DA SERRA: FROM CHOUPANA TO PORTELA

Map begins on pages 60-61, continues on pages 62-63, and ends on pages 80-81; photographs pages 21, 82-83

Distance: See introduction and 'The entire length' below.

Grade: easy throughout, but there is always an initial climb to the levada from the bus stop (except for Short walk 1 in reverse). (The ER202 and ER203 also cross the levada, if friends are willing to play taxi; see map.)

Equipment: stout shoes, sunhat, picnic, water; extra fleece and windproof in cool weather (especially for the stretch north of Camacha)

How to get there and return: See Short walks 1-5 below.

Short walks: See 1-5 below (all are easy).

T he Levada da Serra was our first experience of walking on Madeira, and it may well be yours — especially if you book an 'organised' levada walk. Since much of the way is now signposted, and there is little chance of getting lost, we don't describe the walk in detail. Instead, we tell you how to join the walk at convenient points and do the suggested segments in both directions. *Don't* expect to find much water in this levada — most of it has been diverted to the Tornos, some 200m/650ft below (Walk 7). Nor are there many farreaching views; trees line much of the route. Enjoy instead the flora (hydrangeas, gorse, lilies, rhododendrons) and the pleasant shade of eucalyptus and oak trees. *Do* expect to meet coachloads of walkers …

The **Levada da Serra** is some 27km/17mi long, from the **Lamaceiros** waterhouse above Portela to its end at **Choupana**, northeast of Romeiros. It can be done in one fell swoop, but it breaks conveniently into five short walks.

The entire length: Choupana — Lamaceiros — Portela. 30km/18.6mi; 8h. Grade: moderate (on account of the length). Take *town* 🚍 47 to the Centro Hípico ('**Sehn**-troh **Hee**-pee-koh'). Continue north along the ER201 for 15 minutes, then climb a steep cobbled trail on your right (opposite the Caminho do Meio). In under eight minutes, a short cobbled path on the right leads to the (dry) levada, which may be hidden by tall grass. Follow the levada all the way to the Lamaceiros waterhouse, then pick up Walk 25 to descend to Portela (🚍 53 or 78). Alternatively, leave at the Santo da Serra waterhouse: descend the track on the south side of this waterhouse to the ER102, where you turn right and then left into Santo da Serra for 🚍 20, 77 or 78 (27km/16.7mi; under 8h). If you do this long walk from Portela (see Short walk 5 below), see notes for Short walk 1 to descend from Choupana. *Note: The levada is covered by a road in the Porto Novo Valley; the short walks omit this stretch.*

Short walks

1 Choupana — Achadinha. 7km/4.3mi; 2h10min. Access as 'The entire length'. After crossing the ER203 to Poiso, continue for another 3.5km to Achadinha, where 🚍 111 stops beside the levada. *To walk this leg in reverse,* take 🚍 111 to the Levada da Serra bus stop at Achadinha. Follow the levada west, crossing the ER203 to Poiso. When the levada ends (at Choupana), turn left down the steep cobbled trail to the ER201 (6min). To catch *town* 🚍 47, turn left: in under 15 minutes you'll come to a stop (near the Hortensia tea house). Or carry on to the Jardim Botânico (35min), the cable car at Babosas, or Monte (2h): go straight over the ER201. Descend th steep road ahead 2km to the Jardim Botânico or descend only 500m/yds and then turn right on the Levada dos Tornos. Beyond the Choupana Resort Hotel, at Romeiros (40-45min), steps take you down left off the levada, to avoid a building with a flagpole. You drop 4m/12ft, to a cobbled trail. Turn right on the trail, walking *below* the building with a flagpole. Follow the street lights all the way to Babosas (viewpoint, chapel, cable car terminus) and then Monte.

2   Paradise Valley — Camacha. 6km/3.7mi; 1h40min. Take 🚌 29 or 77 to junction of the ER102 and ER203 at Vale Paraíso ('**Val** Pah-rah-**ee**-soh'). Climb the ER203 towards Poiso to the levada (10min) and turn right. Ignore any forks running down to the right until you come to a junction (about 1h20min), with faded signposts on the left for Choupana and Santo da Serra. Turn right downhill here, to Camacha (🚌 29, 77). *To reverse the walk,* follow the ER102 north from Camacha's square, then climb a road on the left, just past the old church (walkers' signposts on the left). At the levada crossing (under 15min), where a faded signpost indicates 'Choupana', go left. When you come to the crossing Poiso road (ER203) turn down left to the ER102 to catch 🚌 29 or 77. Or carry on to Choupana; for transport from there, see Short walk 1.

3   Águas Mansas — Sítio das Quatro Estradas. 6km/3.7mi; 1h40min. Take 🚌 77 to Águas Mansas, or 🚌 60 or 110 to Boqueirão (from where you must walk 0.6km uphill to the ER102; add 10min). From the joining of the ER206 and the ER102, walk 100m/yds north towards Santo da Serra, then turn left up a road. Past a forestry house, the road reverts to track. Keep left at a fork, then fork right uphill on a path beside the rushing Levada do Pico. You reach the dry Levada da Serra in about 10 minutes. Turn right and follow it as far as the ER202 to Poiso; there turn down right to the ER102 to catch 🚌 77 at the Sítio das Quatro Estradas ('place where four roads join'). *To do this stretch in reverse,* join the levada as in Short walk 4 and turn left. When you reach the noisy Levada do Pico, follow it to the left downhill, to a track. Turn left, then turn right down another track, to the ER102 at Águas Mansas (🚌 77).

4   Sítio das Quatro Estradas — Santo da Serra. 8km/5mi; 2h20min. Take 🚌 77 to the Sítio das Quatro Estradas ('**See**-tee-oh dahs **Kwa**-troh Esh-**trah**-dahsh'). Climb the ER202 towards Poiso. Just beyond a huge piggery (15min), turn right on the levada (*P*10). About 1h15min later, you cross a track and come to the Santo da Serra waterhouse. Enjoy its charming gardens, then return to the track and descend to the ER102 (25min). Turn right downhill, then turn left into Santo da Serra (20min), to catch 🚌 20, 77 or 78. *To do this stretch in reverse,* join the levada as in Short walk 5 and turn left. On reaching the crossing of the ER202 to Poiso, turn down left to the ER102, where you can catch 🚌 77.

5   Santo da Serra — Portela. 8km/5mi; 2h35min. Take 🚌 20, 77 or 78 to Santo da Serra. From the church walk 500m west to the ER102 and turn right uphill for 300m/yds. Then turn left on a road (later a track) and climb 100m/330ft to the Santo da Serra waterhouse. Turn right and walk to the next waterhouse (Lamaceiros). Now follow Walk 25 (map pages 80-81 or 105; notes page 106) to Portela. *To begin at Portela,* walk up the ER102 (signposted to Santo da Serra). Ignore a path right to a shrine but, 150m/yds uphill, climb steps on the right. Follow the narrow Levada da Portela 200m/650ft uphill to the Lamaceiros waterhouse. Walk south on the Levada da Serra to the next waterhouse (Santo da Serra), then descend as in Short walk 4 above.

11 LEVADA DO CANIÇAL: FROM MAROÇOS TO THE CANIÇAL TUNNEL

Map pages 80-81
Distance: 11.5km/7.1mi; 2h40min   **Grade:** easy
Equipment: stout shoes, sunhat, long-sleeved shirt, picnic, water; extra fleece and windproof in cool weather
How to get there: 🚌 156 to Bar Fonte Vermelha (one of the Porto da Cruz or Faial buses coded 'a' in our timetables on page 141)
To return: 🚌 113 from the Pico do Facho bus stop
Short walk: Caniçal tunnel — Boca do Risco — Ribeira Seca. 8.5km/5.3mi; 2h10min. Grade and equipment as above. 🚌 113 to the Pico do Facho bus stop on the western side of the old Caniçal tunnel on the ER109. Join the Levada do Caniçal by the waterhouse on the north side of the road and head west. After 35-40min, you meet the path to Boca do Risco: here a path crosses the levada; it leads up from the last house in the valley (with electricity wires). Follow the path up to the right; it's a 30min climb from here to Boca do Risco (see notes pages 79-80; Walk 14). Return the same way and then descend past the house, following the electricity poles down to the road in the valley. Follow it south to the ER109 at Ribeira Seca, where you can catch 🚌 113.
Alternative walk: Maroços to Caniçal. 16km/10mi; 5h05min. Access as above; grade, equipment, return *as Walk 12.* Do the main walk, then continue to Caniçal by following the first half of Walk 12.

The 'mimosa levada' offers an entrancing and easy walk, accessible to most visitors. If you like, you can extend the walk by including a (1h return) detour to Boca do Risco, or you can tack on Walk 12 — going all the way to Caniçal, or just to Pico do Facho and back. In recent years new housing has burgeoned in the lower valleys, but there are still many peaceful pockets of greenery beside the levada.

The walk begins at **Bar Fonte Vermelha**, where the 156 bus will stop *on request.* (This is just north of the first tunnel on the express road to Porto da Cruz; if approaching by car, see the footnote on page 22.) Across the road is a walkers' signpost for Caniçal. Here you join the **Levada do Caniçal**.

No habitation disturbs the peace in the upper valleys — as yet!

Terracotta birds keep silent watch over the valley of the Ribeira Grande.

Notice the fine basalt prisms on the far side of the valley soon after starting out. You'll quickly gain the narrow **Ribeira das Cales**, as you walk through the strung-out village of Maroços.

Out of this tributary, you pass above a school and then come into the **Ribeira Grande**, crossing the head of the river in **50min**. From now on you will encounter fewer dwellings for a time, but the handiwork of the Madeiran farmer is all around. *Palheiros* dot the landscape, mere specks of red and white in the great bowls of greenery. Perhaps you will meet a youngster bringing home a melon — he puts it into the levada and 'steers' it with a stick … But it is more likely that your only companions will be full-throated frogs singing to their hearts' content.

A short tunnel is met at the end of this valley (**1h**; no torch needed) and two minutes later two waterhouses perched up beside the levada. Then the walk turns into the heavily populated valley of the Ribeira Seca. Take heart! Before pressing on to civilisation we delve into the remote tributary valley shown opposite, the **Ribeira da Noia**. Utterly peaceful, it is still the most beautiful of them all. It soon becomes obvious why we call this the 'mimosa levada'! All year round these golden trees will frame your photographs.

All too soon you regain the great cornucopia of the **Ribeira Seca**. Linger a while beneath some trees; there's a feast for the eyes all around you. From here you can see Machico and the Desertas Islands glimmering in the sun. You cross the main river at a narrow U-turn; about eight minutes later (**2h**), notice a path crossing the levada. It comes up from a house and an electricity pole. This path leads north to Boca do Risco (1h return; notes pages 79-80; Short walk and Walk 14).

Soon you come upon some gorgeous grassy terraces (**P**11), before the way heads back into shade. A waterhouse with brick trellises beside the ER109 marks the end of the walk (**2h40min**); the Caniçal road tunnel is to the left. You can catch a bus here (the Pico do Facho BUS STOP), or at the bar/restaurant O Tonel 350m/yds downhill to the right. Or cross the road and take steps down to a clearly seen trail into Machico (30min). Better still, if you're properly shod and have a head for heights, climb the Pico do Facho road opposite, to tackle Walk 12!

73

12 PICO DO FACHO — CANIÇAL CIRCUIT

Map pages 76-77　　　　　　　　**Distance:** 9km/5.6mi; 3h30min

Grade: moderate, with overall ascents/descents of about 300m/1000ft; you must be sure-footed and have a head for heights (**danger of vertigo**).

Equipment: walking boots, sunhat, long-sleeved shirt, long trousers, picnic, water

How to get there and return: 🚌 113 to/from the Caniçal tunnel: alight at the western end and return from the eastern end. 🚗 By car, park well tucked in at the side of the road to Pico do Facho (or start at Caniçal).

Short walks: Do either half of the main walk, ending at or starting from the church in Caniçal. Grade and equipment as above. About 1h30min.

This invigorating hike first takes you high above the sea, with fine views to São Lourenço. You'll cross grassy terraces veined with old stone walls and then follow an narrow, often precipitous path — once it was a wide mule trail serving the now mostly abandoned terraces. The second half of the walk follows a narrow levada through some delightful woodlands, before making a dramatic descent to the ER109.

Start out at the **Pico do Facho** BUS STOP on the west side of the CANIÇAL TUNNEL. Climb the road towards the peak. Electricity pylons will guide you from here to Caniçal: *take note of them!* The FIRST PYLON comes up just before the peak (**20min**): leave the road here and walk left on a path (almost opposite a trail rising up from Machico). At a Y-fork, bear right. Now you'll see a SECOND PYLON ahead. Your path passes well above it, at the top of some still-cultivated terraces. It takes you straight to the THIRD PYLON (**40min**). Here, on a ridge between the **Ilhéu** and **Pejal** streams, you enjoy first views of Caniçal.

Now the path unexpectedly turns *inland*. Go left up bedrock and after 20 paces fork right. Ten minutes later (**52min**) the FOURTH PYLON is about 150m/yds ahead of you. *Watch out here.* Do *not* follow the path towards this pylon. The path you want (not easily seen at first) turns off to the right and runs about 20m/60ft *below* the pylon and rounds it on the sea side, zigzagging and dropping considerably. When you come to the next bedrock area at a precipice (**1h**), *the path bends sharply to the left.* You overlook Caniçal here. Ten minutes from this precipice, you pass to the left of the FIFTH PYLON (**1h15min**), from where the end of the walk is in view. Looking inland, you spot a beautiful old humpback footbridge over the **Natal** stream below. The path takes you down to it — a scramble involving all fours. Once over the BRIDGE (**1h25min**), take the tarmac road down to the seafront bar and toilets. On the far side of this building, pick up the seafront promenade and follow it left along the coast. Turn left uphill in the centre of **Caniçal**, pass the WHALING MUSEUM, and continue to the OLD CHURCH (**1h40min**; bus stop).

Head east from the church on the main street, then take

the second left turn; Caniçal's large, newer church (with a clock) is ahead on the right. Cross straight over the main road which leads to Baía da Abra; the 'Correos' building will be on your right (**2h**). Climb the road opposite; a green wire fence is on the right. The road soon reverts to track, and the fencing ends, as the track makes for the wood ahead. To mitigate the tedious climb, enjoy the view over right to some wonderful volcanic rock in hues of reds, yellows, golds and greens. Keep beside the gutter at the left of the road; it leads you to the narrow **Levada do Caniçal**, which soon enters a wood full of mimosas (**2h20min**). Follow this small levada as it curves left, away from the track (which continues straight on). Soon you pass a narrower levada rushing down to the left (**2h30min**). Then, from a grassy verge, you have a splendid view down to Caniçal and towards the wind generators on São Lourenço Point.

The same view comes into focus 20 minutes later, this time from the far side of the **Ribeira do Serrado** (see below). Three minutes later you can avoid the awkward levada bridge by using the path in the stream bed below (**2h55min**). Before long the fine buttress of rock formed by the **Lombo do Vento** and **Pico Judeu** rises nearby on your right. A red earthen track crosses the levada, and you leave the woods behind.

With more wide-ranging views you soon near the end of the walk. The levada rounds a bend and now the narrow path runs at the top of a concrete wall high above the ER109 … and below a quarry (**3h15min**). This is a stunning section of the hike. When you come to a concrete track, descend left to the road, where you can *flag down* a BUS (**3h30min**). Motorists should turn right and follow the road through the CANIÇAL ROAD TUNNEL (add 15min; there is a pavement, but this is still *very* unpleasant — it's almost worth taking a bus to the far side!).

São Lourenço Point from the levada path in the Ribeira do Serrado

13 PONTA DE SÃO LOURENÇO

See also photograph page 14 **Distance:** 7km/4.3mi; 2h30min

Grade: moderate, with climbs and descents of about 180m/600ft overall; you should be sure-footed and have a head for heights, to appreciate the precarious viewpoints. The walk runs through a conservation area laid out by the Department of Forestry and Parks; *keep to the designated paths* which are indicated by white waymarking posts and cairns.

Equipment: walking boots, long trousers, long-sleeved shirt, sunhat, picnic, water, whistle; fleece and windproof with hood in cool weather, bathing things in summer

How to get there and return: 🚗 to/from Abra Bay, where the ER109 ends (Car tour 2). Or 🚌 113 to/from Abra Bay (convenient departures; see timetable on page 140 for buses coded 'SL').

Short walk: Abra Bay to the viewpoint over the north coast and return. Easy-moderate, but some people will find the coastal overlook vertiginous; 35 minutes return; *especially recommended* as a leg-stretcher on Car tour 2. Stout shoes, sunhat. Access as main walk. Follow the main walk for 20min, then return to the car park.

The sun-tanned arm of São Lourenço Point beckons you when you first approach the island by air. Whether you're an experienced walker or just a novice, *do* spend a day out here. Not only are there wonderful flora — including the ice plant (*Mesembryanthemum crystallinum*), but extraordinary geological formations — basalt intrusions into sandstone, uptilted magma dykes which can be traced across the terrain, metamorphosed sandstone with astonishing textures and colours, and eroded soft rock under basalt tors. You also come almost face-to-face with the full fury of the Atlantic thrashing against the coast and offshore rocks.

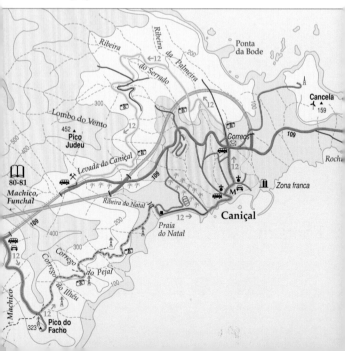

Start the walk where the ER109 ends, at tranquil **Abra Bay** (**Baía da Abra**; *P*13). Circle to the right of the knoll, walking below and to the right of the picnic tables. You enjoy a fine view of the lighthouse at the end of the point, the eyelet in the lighthouse rock, and the Desertas Islands. Notice the lovely strata opposite you, on the far side of Abra Bay. You can also spot your ongoing route: an earthen track heading along the arm of the peninsula, on the south side of a hill with fencing and the Pedras Brancas trig stone. After rounding the knoll, drop down to this track using one of the many paths, then head east. Go through a gap in an old stone wall (**10min**) and then come upon wonderful views (**15min**; *P*13): to the right is Abra Bay and to the left the north coast headlands as far west as São Jorge. Soon, at a fork, go left, coming to a lip of rock on the north coast in half a minute (**20min**). Here you overlook the magnificent 'sea horse' rocks shown on page 14. The colours are astounding: they seem almost fluorescent, so intense is their purple-red colour as they thrust up from a turquoise-to-indigo sea.

Return to the fork and head left, climbing a path and bedrock. *(But for the Short walk, turn right at the fork, back to the car park.)* At a pass (**25min**), *be sure to follow the posts and cairns*, which lead back north to another viewpoint over the north coast 'sea horse' rocks (**30min**) and crosses a saddle where there are more fine views to the left.

Some **40min** into the hike the character of the walk changes completely; the path is clearly seen, and you might like to take a break at a sheltered, grassy spot.

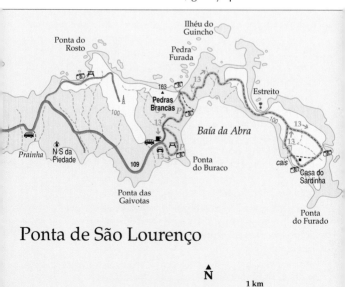

Ponta de São Lourenço

Ponta de São Lourenço

Seven minutes later (**47min**) you come to a stone marker, 'TC/75', at the **Estreito** (straits), which used to be notoriously difficult to negotiate. From the marker walk 90° left over bedrock, until you overlook the north side of the point. Then follow the sturdy metal fencing, descending in zigzags back to the main path.

From here on the going is really easy and totally exhilarating. Flora are under recovery in this area; *please keep to the paths* defined by the rockery stones. Ahead in the valley is the park rangers' house (CASA DO SARDINHA). On reaching a fork (**1h**), you can decide whether to make a clockwise or anti-clockwise circuit round the house.* Whichever route you choose, you will pass two cliff-side viewpoints looking out to the rest of the peninsula and the Ilhéu do Farol with its lighthouse; these shreds of land are only accessible from the sea. En route you can stop at the little quay (CAIS DO SARDINHA) for a swim or a picnic — or maybe even help the rangers bring some supplies ashore.

The park rangers do not mind a couple of picnickers enjoying a break in the shade of palms at the house, but they would certainly not appreciate a group! If you are lucky enough not to be surrounded by dozens of walkers, ask them first and *leave **no** litter*. It's so romantic, you might even be tempted to try Eve's trick and share an apple with your mate. The house and quay were built in the early 1900s by a businessman from Funchal called Sardinha.

From here retrace your route, carefully following the way-marking posts and cairns over the bedrock. You'll be back at the CAR PARK in about **2h30min**. There is usually a refreshment van here.

*The hill beyond the house, which featured in earlier editions of this book, is now a conservation area and *out of bounds.*

14 NORTH COAST PATH: CANIÇAL TUNNEL • BOCA DO RISCO • PORTO DA CRUZ

Distance: 13km/8mi; 4h

Grade: moderate, with total ascents of about 200m/650ft and descents of 400m/1300ft, but you must be sure-footed and have a head for heights (**danger of vertigo**). The path, 350m/1150ft above the sea, is narrow, often slippery, and **prone to landslides** (usually between Boca do Risco and Espigão Amarelo, below Pico Larano). Organised walking tours use this route regularly, and fencing *usually* protects the worst stretches (but it often comes down in storms).

Equipment: walking boots, sunhat, long trousers, long-sleeved shirt, picnic, water, whistle, fleece, windproof with hood

How to get there: 🚌 113 to the Pico do Facho bus stop
To return: 🚌 53, 56 or 78 from Porto da Cruz

Short walk: See Short walk 11 on page 72.

Alternative walk: Larano — Espigão Amarelo — Porto da Cruz. 7.5km/4.7mi; 2h50min. Fairly easy, but you must be sure-footed and have a head for heights (**danger of vertigo**). Equipment, return as above. Access: 🚌 53, 56, 78 or 103 to Porto da Cruz, then taxi to Larano, where the tarred road ends. Or use the map to walk up to Larano — allow about 1h. (🚗: You can also refer to the map overleaf to drive there and walk along the coastal path as long as you like.) At Larano the start of the walk is signalled by a sign with an orange rectangle and three stars: follow this concrete-surfaced road for some 800m to the coastal path, which you meet above Cova das Pedras. Follow the path to Espigão Amarelo, where there is a stone marker ('JMG'). Or follow it all the way to Boca do Risco, from where you could join Short walk 11. To return to Porto da Cruz from Larano, pick up the notes for the main walk at the 3h20min-point. *NB: see also Alternative walk 15, for a different approach to Larano.*

This is a walk of contrasts. Amble along the Levada do Caniçal, marvelling at the sun-blessed fertility of Madeira's soil. You can forget for a while what it has cost the islanders in toil, for there are few tiny terraces here, just

West of Espigão Amarelo your coastal views are framed by pines. Here's where you will see banks of pink belladonna lilies in the autumn.

lush farmland. Then climb from the levada to the crest of the coast. Here the wind wakes you to the cruel realities of life on the island. The north coast between Boca do Risco and Porto da Cruz is perhaps the quintessence of Madeira — nowhere else on the island can match its rugged, proud beauty in sunlight; few places in the world could match its harsh anger when lashed by storms.

Begin the walk at the PICO DO FACHO BUS STOP on the west side of the CANIÇAL ROAD TUNNEL. Cross the road and find the **Levada do Caniçal** (see Walk 11) beside the waterhouse. Follow the levada northwest for about **35-40min**, until you come to a path crossing the levada. It leads diagonally up from a house and electricity poles below on the left. Follow the path uphill to the right. The climb is gradual at first, through farmland; you are heading towards the saddle which can be seen above. Later brush and bilberry take over, leading to forests of mimosa and pine. The air is delicious and fresh, with just a hint of salt blowing in from the sea. Within **1h10min** you reach the lip of the coast at **Boca do Risco** (the 'dangerous gap'). Here are houseleeks like great cabbages, snowball trees, thistles, gorse, ferns, laurel, heath and wild flowers in every colour imaginable. Off across the sea to the northeast, Porto Santo may be clearly visible.

Turn left to make for Porto da Cruz on a path that will be quite narrow in places (the old weather-beaten sign shows an orange rectangle with two stars.) As you progress, look back east for a view of the Ilhéu do Guincho ('Screech Islet') — so called because the wind shrieks through its tiny eyelet. This is one of our favourite views … dazzling in morning sun or glimmering in afternoon glow. Then new headlands come into view and, by **2h20min**, you'll reach a promontory with a stone marker ('JMG') just above the **Espigão Amarelo** ('Sharp Yellow Point') … a splendid lunch spot. As you take a break here, you may be as awe-struck as we are by the fencing the shepherds have built below the path and down the cliffs. Even more baffling is the narrow strip of cultivated terraces in the east, stretching almost all the way from the cliff-top down to the sea on what looks like a 60° slope!

The character of the coastal path changes dramatically beyond the stone marker, its starkness soon softened by pine forests and, in the autumn, banks of pink belladonna lilies. You look down to a sea of palest turquoise through pine trees standing tall in ochre-red soil. The waves break over the rocks below again and again and again, creating endless patterns of the finest lace. Before long you catch your first views of Porto da Cruz, huddled below Eagle Rock. In the foreground, a dinosaur's back of a ridge thrusts out into the sea.

By this time a concrete road has come underfoot, and at **3h05min** the road leaves the cliff. You descend into a valley with emerald crops and laden vines, where you eventually join an asphalt road (**3h20min**). This is **Larano**. Follow the road downhill. In 10 minutes, it bends sharply left. Straight ahead you'll see a small hill with access doors to hillside storage caves. Leave the road here, descending concrete steps to the right. You pass to the left of the caves on a stone-laid path which then takes you down to a road. Cross over and turn right for 15m/yds, then go left down a track. A causeway* takes you over the mouth of the **Ribeira da Maiata** (**3h40min**). Now just follow the coastal promenade into **Porto da Cruz** (**4h**). The BUS STOP is uphill, on the main ER108, in front of the Centro de Saúde.

*We are unsure whether a bridge will eventually be built here. Should the causeway be flooded (only likely after a severe winter storm), you will have to follow the road above the river to the left for 500m/yds, back to the Larano road. Turn right here, then turn right on the road to Porto da Cruz (add 35-40 minutes). From the road there is a fine view of your destination, focusing on its rock, old sugar refinery and church.

15 FROM PORTELA TO PORTO DA CRUZ

Map pages 80-81   **Distance:** 6km/3.7mi; 1h55min

Grade: moderate descent of 600m/1970ft, of which 300m is very steep. You must be sure-footed. The trail is slippery in wet weather.

Equipment: walking boots, long trousers, sunhat, water, walking stick

How to get there: 🚌 53 or 78 to Portela

To return: 🚌 53, 56 or 78 from Porto da Cruz

Alternative walk: Portela — Larano — Alternative walk 14. 12km/7.4mi; 4h40min. Grade, access as above. Follow the main walk until it turns down left to the causeway. Just 15m/yds *before* this track, climb an old stone-laid path on the right. Concrete steps take you up to a road: turn left to Larano (2h) and do Alternative walk 14 on page 79.

In the 1800s the *borracheiros* used this trail to transport wine, carried in goatskins on their backs, from Porto da Cruz to the south. Visually stunning in its own right, this walk is an ideal approach to Alternative walk 14.

Begin at **Portela**: head east on the lane skirting the north side of the restaurant 'MIRADOURO DA PORTELA'. After 200m/yds (*P*15), turn left on an old stone-laid trail signposted 'CAMINO MUNICIPAL'). Zigzag steeply down, enjoying the superb view shown below. When the trail forks, go left, passing a water storage tank on your left. The trail becomes tarred and you meet a crossing road (**40min**). Turn right for about 15m/yds, then swing sharp left down a minor road. Continue steeply downhill through the strung-out village of **Cruz da Guarda**.

When you reach a T-junction by the **Ribeira da Maiata** (**1h25min**), turn right, cross the bridge, then take the first left turn. After 150m (just before a school), turn left again. Follow this road for 500m/yds along the east side of the river. Then take a track down left, cross a causeway (see footnote opposite!), and follow the coastal promenade into **Porto da Cruz** (**1h55min**).

Strung-out villages straddle the ridges between Portela and Eagle Rock.

Map pages 80-81, then 105   **Distance:** 9km/5.6mi; 2h50min

Grade: easy (ascent/descent of under 100m/330ft), but you must be sure-footed and have a head for heights.

Equipment: walking boots, long trousers, sunhat, picnic, water

How to get there and return: 🚐 53 or 78 to/from Cruz, or 🚗: park at the tiny electricity substation at Cruz, east of Faial (there are small parking bays either side and a bar/café opposite).

Alternative walk: Levada Nova — Levada do Castelejo — Cruz. 12km/7.4mi; 3h30min. Grade, equipment, return as above. 🚐 53 or 78 to the Achada turn-off ('ish-**trah**-dah pah-rah Ah-**shah**-dah'). From the bus stop, walk down the main road past the 'Referta' sign as far as the road to Cruz da Guarda on the right. Pick up the Levada Nova here, below the road on the *left,* and follow its sluggish flow towards Penha de Águia, through the pretty, but extraordinarily named valley of Tem-te Não Caias ('Hold on; watch you don't fall!'). Some 50min along, cross straight over a cobbled trail to join the main walk (at the 10min-point).

U tter bliss! Following a narrow levada, in just over an hour you move from the cornucopia of cultivation below Penha de Águia into the wilderness of the Ribeiro Frio, with its limpid pools, mimosas and ancient fine-leaved laurels.

Start the walk at **Cruz**, a few paces uphill from the ELECTRI-CITY SUBSTATION. Almost opposite the 'Cruz' sign there are two roads: climb the road on the right (signpost: 'LEVADA DO CASTELEJO'), passing a bar/shop on your right immediately. At a Y-fork (**5min**), *keep left* (even though 'Levada do Castelejo' is signposted both left and right. Within **10min** you come to the **Levada do Castelejo**, on your right. *(The Alternative walk comes in here, from the left.)* Turn right, walking against the current. Lime-green vines will frame your photographs of Penha de Águia, São Roque and Faial.

Beyond a road crossing (**20min**), you round a promontory and soon see Faial's church down to the right. São Roque's church, on the next *lombo,* seems close enough to touch. Then you turn sharp left up the magnificent valley of the **Ribeira de São Roque** (*P*16). In **40min** the levada channel is but a ribbon on the escarpment, but steel railings and wires afford at least psychological protection. Other drops are encountered further on, but they are all masked by scrub, and the path is always at least 60cm/2ft wide.

In **1h25min** you're at the levada's source; stone steps take you down to the boulder-strewn **Ribeiro Frio**. The pools are so clear that you might be tempted to swim. Only birdsong disturbs the peace of this primeval place.

From here return to **Cruz** (**2h50min**).

Walks 16 and 17 look out over São Roque and across the Metade and Seca valleys to the high peaks.

17 PENHA DE ÁGUIA

Map pages 80-81   **Distance:** 3km/1.9mi; 2h30min

Grade: a strenuous climb of 450m/1475ft and descent of 350m/1150ft. The upward path is diabolically slippery, with grit, loose soil and pine needles underfoot. *Only recommended for very experienced walkers and only advisable in summer,* when local walkers will have hacked a way through the dense foliage. **Danger of vertigo!**

Equipment: walking boots, sunhat, long-sleeved shirt, long trousers, picnic, water, whistle, walking stick; extra fleece and windproof in cool weather

How to get there: 🚌 53, 56 or 78 to Porto da Cruz, then taxi to the Restaurante Galé in Penha de Águia de Baixo; or 🚗 to Penha de Águia de Baixo (the turn-off is just east of the São Roque River; Car tour 4); park near the Restaurante Galé.
To return: 🚌 53 or 78 from Cruz — back to your base, or to the Penha de Águia de Baixo turn-off, from where you can walk back to your car (add 1.1km/20min).

Alternative ascent from Cruz: To climb and descend the same way, begin at Cruz (grade and equipment as above, but saves 100m of ascent). Take 🚌 53 or 78 to Cruz (or 🚗; park as for Walk 16 opposite). Some 20m/yds below (east of) the sub-station, cross the road and walk up the lane on the *right-hand side of the café* (*ignore* the signpost 'Vereda da Penha d'Águia' opposite the sign for the Levada do Castelejo). After just a few metres/yards, turn right in front of a house, on a very narrow and overgrown path (just past the house there will be a narrow levada on your left). Your path up the mountain begins 230m/yds along this path; it rises very steeply on the left (*no* waymarking). Once on the top, climb left for 10 minutes to the triangulation stone. Return the same way.

W hen we first did this hike, we were torn to shreds by the most impenetrable jungle of lacerating ferns, gorse and blackberries we'd ever encountered. The secret is to do it in summer or early autumn, after the holiday season has started for the young Madeiran walkers. Unless they precede you with their machetes, you won't even *find* the uphill path,

let alone enjoy the views! Since this hike is only recommended for *very experienced walkers,* we have not described the zigs and zags in detail.

Start out at **Penha de Águia de Baixo**: climb concrete steps between the Restaurante Galé on the left and a house on the right. Immediately beyond the buildings, take the very narrow path ahead, through high grass. At a Y-fork (**2min**), bear left towards a *palheiro,* passing it three minutes later. There is a fine view back to Faial from here. Beyond the cow-house the narrow path turns left towards the sea. You stumble through blackberries and over broken stretches of path. Sometimes you will lose the path as it crosses bedrock. *Always keep an eye open for unexpected zigzags and aim for the 'dip' between the two 'summits' above.* The path climbs the right-hand side of a densely wooded ravine which opens out 300m/1000ft above the sea in a small waterfall (hidden from view).

In **55min** you reach the top of the rock's western ridge at a fork: to the right are views down to the sea; ahead is an abyss. Go left, following the ridge and skirting the valley below on the left. Five minutes later you are just above the road to Penha de Águia de Baixo, and this is the best part of the walk. The path, coated with pine needles, is wide and almost level, and there are superb views below on the right, focusing on São Roque and the Metade and Seca valleys, with the high peaks as a backdrop.

Beyond this lovely 'user-friendly' section comes the most unpleasant part of the walk. Even if young Madeirans have hacked out the path for you, you will need all fours to haul yourself steeply up over broken tree roots. It seems never-ending, but you finally stagger up to the trig point at the top of **Penha de Águia** (589m/1930ft) in **1h30min**. Now, whenever you are on the north coast, you can look up to this tall white pillar and say with justifiable satisfaction: *I did it!*

Continue along the lip of the mountainside, past the pillar. In seven minutes you will come to a pass (550m/1800ft) and a rock outcrop on the right. The path descending from here is far better than the ascent route. Zigzag down, sometimes through pines, for about 50 minutes. You will eventually drop down to a narrow levada; turn right along it. On coming to houses, turn left down to the ER108 at **Cruz** (**2h30min**), where you will find a bar/café on your right. The Funchal bus stops at the electricity sub-station opposite the bar/café or, if you have left your car at the start of the walk, catch a Faial-bound bus in front of the café and ask the conductor for '**Pain**-yah day **Ah**-gee-ah, Rish-toh-**rahnt** Gah-**lay**'. Alight at the bridge over the São Roque River and climb the road back to your car (add 20 minutes).

18 SANTANA • SÃO JORGE • VIGIA

Cover photograph   **Distance:** 10.5km/6.5mi; 3h30min

Grade: moderate-strenuous, with over 400m/1300ft of descents and corresponding ascents. *Not recommended in damp weather, when the trails would be slippery, or in strong winds.*

Equipment: walking boots, raingear, windproof, fleece, long trousers, swimwear, sunhat, picnic, water

How to get there: 🚌 103 or 138 (Arco bus); ask for '**Vail**-yoh So-**lahr**' (the old *solar*); the stop is 1.7km northwest of Santana's town hall (150m north of Bragados Restaurant), 400m south of the Quinta do Furão road. By 🚗: park in São Jorge and take 🚌 103 or 138 to the start.
To return: 🚌 103 from the Vigia turn-off at São Jorge; *be there at least 10min before departure time from São Jorge.*

Shorter walk: Santana — São Jorge. 7.5km/4.7mi; 2h37min. Grade, equipment, access/return as above. End the walk at São Jorge's church.

An old zigzag trail, high cliffs, the throbbing sea beside you … this walk was made in heaven. And if you're heartbroken when it ends, just turn to page 41. Explore the island's remaining old cobbled trails *now*, before they're bulldozed out of existence…

To start the walk, climb the cobbled road on the north side of the 'SOLAR' BUS STOP, passing flower-filled gardens. In **4min** you come to a rosy-pink *solar,* one of the island's early manors, now in ruins. Fork right in front of the entrance, curving below the building on a cobbled trail, overlooking the **Achada do Gramacho**, a small plain laced with vines. On reaching a tarred road at the QUINTA DO FURÃO, turn left and walk up 10m/yds, to where 'Stop' is written on the road, then turn right. Follow the road for some 700m/0.5mi; it skirts to the west of a conical hill, the **Cabeço da Vigia**. Just before you reach the highest point in the road, where there is a stand of pines on the left and a blue sign, 'SÃO JORGE, CALHAU', go left down an earthen track. Soon the old cobbled trail shown on page 29 is visible beneath the iron-rich soil.

You've begun the exhilarating descent into the **Ribeira de São Jorge**. The setting is magnificent: the great peaks rise inland while, ahead of you, São Jorge's church and light-house glimmer brightly above a blue, blue sea. On the far side of the valley, you can see your old cobbled trail up to São Jorge; it begins by some cottages snuggled amidst tiny banana groves. Another path skirts the coast.

All too soon the descent ends; at **1h** you're crossing the old bridge by a new bathing area. Turn right and follow the coastal path, past a shop/bar on the left and a beautifully kept house beside the banana groves. Just beyond it are the few remains of **Calhau**, once such an important port that it boasted both a church *and* a chapel! Part of an old wall, with remnants of tiles, still rises near the sea. Opposite the first of the ruins is a tap and the trail we'll climb later to São Jorge.

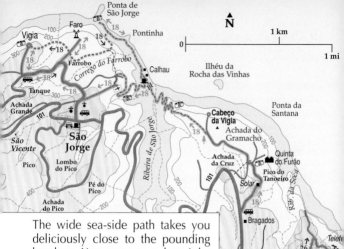

The wide sea-side path takes you deliciously close to the pounding breakers. You come to a deep inlet just below the lighthouse (**1h20min**); ahead is a fishermen's bridge over to the **Ponta de São Jorge**. This bridge is often damaged by rock falls; enjoy the view *from a distance!**

Return to Calhau (**1h40min**), for a picnic in the emerald grass, then turn up the steep trail by the tap. As you climb, look across to your descending trail, etched into the cliff on the far side of the river. By **2h15min** you will have huffed and puffed up to a junction. Cross half-left over the road and climb cobbled steps towards the cream-coloured walls of São Jorge's cemetery. Facing the cemetery gate (**2h25min**), turn right up a road, after seven minutes passing a chapel on the left. Continue round left to visit the magnificent baroque church in the centre of **São Jorge** (**2h37min**). Nearby are a bar and a BUS STOP. (*The Shorter walk ends here.*)

Walk back to the palm-shaded chapel and turn left. Ignore a road off right; continue ahead along the ESTRADA MUNICIPAL DO FARROBO. Beyond a stream (**Corrego do Farrobo**), climb to a T-junction and turn right to visit the LIGHTHOUSE (**3h**). Then return to the *estrada municipal* and turn right. At a three-way junction turn right to the **Vigia**, a viewpoint reached five minutes later (**3h25min**). From here the views west capture the attention, especially over Ponta Delgada's seaside church on a flat spit of land and the huge hotel, with Cabanas above and Ribeira da Janela in the distance. Now return to the Estrada Municipal do Farrobo (**3h30min**) — you can flag down a bus at the VIGIA SIGNPOST. (It's a good idea to arrive 10 minutes early, to be on the safe side!)

*A old trail from here up to the Vigia has recently been cleared; you may like to climb it, then walk on to São Jorge.

19 PICO DO ARIEIRO • PICO RUIVO • ACHADA DO TEIXEIRA

Map on reverse of touring map; see also photographs pages 4, 28, 93

Distance: 6km/3.7mi; 3h10min

Grade: very strenuous, with steep ascents (about 550m/1800ft overall) and descents (about 700m/2300ft overall). You must be sure-footed and have a head for heights; **danger of vertigo.** Five tunnels en route (20min total). *Sometimes the walk is impassable due to landslides or snowfall.*

Equipment: walking boots, raingear, windproof, fleece, long trousers, whistle, sunhat, picnic, plastic bottle/water purifying tablets, torch, walking stick

How to get there and return: 🚕 taxi to Pico do Arieiro and back from the Achada do Teixeira (or with friends who are touring; Car tour 4)

Short walk: Pico do Arieiro — first or second viewpoint — Pico do Arieiro. 35min-1h15min. Stout shoes, sunhat. Moderate ups and downs on hundreds of steps; you must be sure-footed and fairly agile; **possibility of vertigo.** Access/return: 🚕 car or taxi to Pico do Arieiro.

Alternative walks

1 Pico do Arieiro — Pico Ruivo via the Torres. 10km/6.2mi; 4h15min. Grade as main walk, but ascents and descents of about 750m/2500ft overall. One 100m-long tunnel. Although this route is waymarked and mostly protected with fencing, these slopes are prone to landslides. Unless you are a very confident hiker, used to 'exposure', consider doing this walk with an organised group. Follow the main walk through Pico do Gato (45min), then fork right through the gate. After a short downward stretch, the *real* climbing begins, over hundreds of badly worn steps. It takes a good 45 minutes to reach the pass on the eastern shoulder of the Torres (1800m/5900ft; 1h30min). Beyond the pass, the path curves left and descends in zigzags and more steps. Finally (2h20min) you come to a junction, where the fifth (final) tunnel of the main route is on your left. Pick up the main walk just after the 1h15min-point.

2 Pico do Arieiro — Pico Ruivo — Queimadas — Santana. 16km/10mi; 6h. *Only possible after a long period of dry weather.* Equipment and access as main walk; add another 1200m/3900ft of steep descent. A route for masochistic experts! Do the main walk, then cross the car park at the Achada. Go to the front of the building and walk past it. Below you will spot the basaltic dyke shown on page 93, Homem em Pé. Descend to the right of it and continue down to the road not far below. Follow the road a short way downhill to a viewpoint, from where the path continues (at the left side). *From here on the very steep clay path can be as slippery as ice.* Hang on to heath trees where you can, and take a walking stick! Some 1h20min from the Achada, go through a gate and soon reach the upper house in the story-book setting of Queimadas Park. From the lower house (1h30min) take the steep cobbled road down to Santana (allow 1h30min). Turn right on the main road: buses leave from the town hall (the building with a clock).

3 Pico do Arieiro — Pico Ruivo — Torrinhas — Curral. 13.5km/8.4mi; 6h15min. Add another 1000m/3300ft of steep descent. Do the main walk and, at Pico Ruivo, pick up Alternative walk 20 on page 92.

Try to make a *very* early morning start and get to Pico do Arieiro at daybreak. The sun erupts like a ball of fire; shards of light cascade mauve and golden over mountaintops and valleys. The mists clear quickly but reluctantly,

*Do start out as early as possible. This photograph was taken at about 10.30, just below Pico do Arieiro. The mists are already descending, obscuring the first viewpoint (to the right) and the Torres peaks behind it. Pico do Cidrão is the attractive red wedge on the left, at the head of the Cidrão and Metade ravines. Built in the late 1960s, Madeira's most famous mountain path is very well engineered, and the difficult stretches are protected by sturdy wire fencing. The fences sometimes come down in storms — or land-slides block the tunnels, but this route is now so popular that repairs are made fairly quickly. If you are unlucky enough to walk just after a landslide, **please use good judgement and turn back.***

curling lovingly around the peaks, mere wisps and whispers and then they're gone. A shepherd appears suddenly from beneath a crest, shouldering a heavy load of firewood, sending goats and sheep scurrying between light and shade, as fluffy clouds throw shadows across the scrubby slopes.

The photograph on page 119 gives you a good overview of the ups and downs of your route. Here on Madeira's third highest peak (1818m/5965ft), you are far above the great Cidrão and Metade ravines. Most mornings the air is so clear that you can see to the heights above Porto Moniz.

Start the walk at **Pico do Arieiro**: follow the paved path shown above. You cross a very narrow spine — a foretaste of the great chasms to follow on this trail linking the island's three highest mountains. The ups and downs begin almost at once, as you struggle over a massive knoll protruding from the spine and then descend to a grassy verge (**P**19), a fine picnic spot. In **15min** you reach the first viewpoint along the route, the **Miradouro Ninho da Manta** (Buzzard's Nest), from where there is a good view down to Fajã da Nogueira, setting for Walk 24. From here you can also discern, to the northwest, a path around the east side of the **Torres**, the island's second highest mountain (Alternative walk 1). The jagged teeth crowning this 'Peak of the Towers' hide Ruivo from view for most of the walk. But you *can* see the island's highest peak — and, on a clear day, the outskirts of

Funchal — from the second viewpoint, reached in **25min**.

In **30min** a steep descent on yet more steps begins; at the end of this descent, a ROCK ARCH will frame your photographs. Follow the path through the arch and soon look right to get splendid views over the Metade Valley and the village of São Roque perched on its *lombo*.

A FIRST TUNNEL is met in **45min**; it passes through the isolated needle of **Pico do Gato** ('Cat's Peak'). Beyond this tunnel, a gate on the right leads to Alternative walk 1; keep *left* here, unless a sign warns that the tunnels ahead are closed. (This stretch, scene of frequent landslides, is potentially the most hazardous.) Go on into the second tunnel (**1h**). The third and fourth tunnels follow immediately. Just past the fourth, a grassy, broom-bedecked knoll commands spectacular views to Pico Grande and the Paúl da Serra.

Enter the FIFTH AND LAST TUNNEL in **1h15min**. At its exit, the Torres path (Alternative walk 1) comes in from the right. The ongoing path to Pico Ruivo now skirts a cliff-edge with some caves. Soon the way is very like the trail between Ruivo and Encumeada (Walk 20): the broom gives way to gnarled heath trees which grace sweeping vistas over the Metade.

It's a tiresome slog up to the Ruivo REST HOUSE (under **2h**), where you may be able to buy a drink. After tackling the SUMMIT OF **Pico Ruivo** (**2h10min**), follow the paved path from the rest house down to the **Achada do Teixeira** (**3h10min**).

20 ACHADA DO TEIXEIRA • PICO RUIVO • TORRINHAS • ENCUMEADA

Map on reverse of touring map   **Distance:** 18km/11.2mi; 6h25min

Grade: very strenuous, with overall ascents of 550m/1800ft and descents of 1100m/3600ft. The walk is waymarked throughout with red and yellow flashes. You must be sure-footed and have a head for heights; **danger of vertigo.** *Avoid the walk in wet weather, when the hundreds of stone steps are slippery.* Expect to be caught up in mists. We have never encountered landslides en route, but don't discount the possibility. You must walk quickly, too; bus times are very tight! ***Important note:*** Several paths radiate north and south from this walk, but only the routes described are used regularly. *Experts* may wish to tackle some of the others (which we mention in passing), but we would not recommend any of them and so have not highlighted them in colour on our map.

Equipment: walking boots, raingear, windproof, fleece, long trousers, whistle, compass, sunhat, picnic, plastic bottle/water purifying tablets, walking stick

How to get there: 🚌 56, 103 or 138 to Santana or 🚌 53, 56, 78 or 103 to Faial, then taxi to the Achada do Teixeira. You will have to walk faster than our times to catch 🚌 6! Consider staying overnight in Santana, to give you time to *savour* this walk; you might even start at sunrise, as we do (arrange this with a taxi in advance).
To return: 🚌 6 from Encumeada (or telephone from the bar at Encumeada for a Ribeira Brava taxi and take a later bus from Ribeira Brava).

Short walk: Achada do Teixeira — Pico Ruivo — Achada do Teixeira. 5.5km/3.4mi; 1h50min. Moderate climb and descent of 270m/900ft on a stone-paved path (with shelters and springs en route). Stout shoes, fleece, windproof, sunhat, picnic, water. Access: as above (ask the taxi driver to wait for you or to return for you), or by 🚗 (Car tour 4).

Alternative walk: Achada do Teixeira — Pico Ruivo — Torrinhas — Curral. 16km/10mi; 5-6h. Access, equipment, grade as above (but a further 400m/1300ft of very steep descent, on a path often covered with slippery eucalyptus leaves). Do the main walk and, at Torrinhas Pass, descend the path waymarked in red and yellow flashes. You reach the bridge over the Ribeira do Curral 1h45min below Torrinhas; this is Fajã dos Cardos. Follow the road to the right for 20min, to Colmeal (just over 5h), where you can catch 🚌 81, or climb up to Curral (6h; 🚌 81).

Blood red, then mauve; and finally silver and blue and gold. All was shadow; all was light. Nothing was real. Where sky ended and sea began, where mountains soared and clouds tiptoed down — all was merged into one. Sunrise at Pico Ruivo, the ideal time to start this walk.

   Start out at the **Achada do Teixeira** (*P*20). First walk behind the house to admire the view shown opposite, then head west on the paved ridge path to Pico Ruivo; you'll pass some springs and shelters on the way. About **40min** up, you enjoy wonderful views of Arieiro, the Torres and the path of Walk 19. This path from Arieiro comes in from the left, and you quickly reach the government REST HOUSE below Pico Ruivo (**45min**; refreshments sometimes available).

   Five minutes above the house, you'll come to a saddle and a sign indicating that this path was built in 1949 and that it is 16km from here to Encumeada. At the left are steps to the summit of **Pico Ruivo** (1862m/6105ft; **55min**), with its twin viewpoints. You'll want to linger up here to see how many landmarks you can spot, including the Pico das Torres, Torrinhas Pass, Pico Grande, the Paúl da Serra, the Metade and Curral valleys, and the *pousadas* at Queimadas. To the northeast Porto Santo floats like a cloud on the horizon.

From the summit, return to the sign and turn down left for Encumeada. As the well-waymarked red earthen path descends the northwestern flanks of Ruivo, take the opportunity to climb up slightly to the right, to see the fantastic views over the north coast, about 1300m/4250ft below. Twenty minutes below the saddle, you pass through a gate. Now the valley leading down to Curral das Freiras opens up before you almost at once, and you can see the higher hamlet of Fajã dos Cardos (on the route of the Alternative walk).

In **1h40min** come to a particularly good viewpoint over Curral's setting; now the path dips down south for a while, before resuming its westerly course. In **1h55min** start climbing to skirt a cone-shaped sandstone peak on your right … all the while enjoying the perfume of wild mint and thyme crushed underfoot.

At **2h05min** you'll reach a promontory with chasms to the left. Here, a disused path to Curral via Lombo Grande goes straight ahead; we go to the right. At **2h25min** climb down some steps and into another valley, from where you can again see the north coast. You may also spot another derelict path, this one leading down right to São Jorge via Pico Canário, just before Pico das Eirinhas. Already you can see across the great valleys of the Ribeira Brava and São Vicente rivers, which split the island in two, and the

Homem em Pé ('Man on Foot'), an impressive basaltic dyke just below the Achada do Teixeira house. From here there is a fine view down over the São Jorge Valley (Picnic 20; Alternative walk 19-1).

pronounced hairpins of the road from Miradouro (Walk 29) to the Paúl da Serra.

In **2h45min**, find a perfect promontory for lunch. Here two or three people can sit wedged in nature's rock-chairs and picnic overlooking Curral das Freiras. This is just before you reach a fork (where there *may* still be a large painted stone). Here a clear path descends left to Curral, but this is *not* the path we recommend for the Alternative walk. We head up *right* here. The most hazardous section of the walk is soon encountered: not far beyond a gate, back on the north side of the ridge, the path descends about a dozen steep and slippery stone steps beside a precipice. The wire railings here are often in disrepair. *Stow everything away before you make this potentially dangerous descent...* and watch your footing on the very slippery section that follows. Then reach a grassy verge overlooking the north coast — an ideal picnic spot for groups of walkers.

Soon you are confronted by the first of *many* flights of steep stone steps. These lead up to **Torrinhas Pass** (**3h**), where signs point the way to Curral, Pico Ruivo, and Encumeada. (*The Alternative route descends to the left here.*) You may also see a sign pointing to the threadbare remains of the old (1800s) trail to Boaventura; it too, is derelict, and its lower reaches have succumbed to the asphalt of the ER108. The path now takes you over the shoulders of **Pico do Jorge** — forever up and forever down — a climb and descent of over 200m/650ft lasting almost an hour, on giant-sized steps.

Beyond a signposted SPRING on the left (**4h30min**), a rock arch frames your photographs of the valleys of Serra de Água and São Vicente. Then descend through a glen of giant ferns beside a basalt escarpment at **Pico do Ferreiro**. At **4h55min** you may see a steep path down left: it is part of a 1800s trail to the Jardim da Serra via Pico Grande. We know of a couple of *experts* who have walked it, but we have *not*.

This part of the walk, west of Pico do Jorge, can be glorious. But mists frequently descend by early afternoon, obscuring the valleys. Mist will be a boon for those who suffer from vertigo: the hundreds *and hundreds* of STONE STEPS on which you descend 300m/1000ft to the end of the walk seem to spiral in space, but in heavy mist the abyss is not apparent, and all you can see are the many nearby *folhados* (wild lily of the valley trees). Fortunately the steps are amply wide!

Eventually a steep dirt track takes you to the ER228 at **Encumeada** (1004m/3293ft; **6h25min**). Walk 31 can begin here, at the *miradouro* over the São Vicente Valley. Follow the road south over the pass, to find the SIGN TO FOLHADAL beside the **Levada do Norte**, starting point for Walk 32. Wait here for the BUS, or telephone for a taxi from the bar.

21 PICO DAS PEDRAS • COVA DA RODA • CRUZINHAS

Map pages 98-99   **Distance:** 8.5km/5.3mi; 2h35min

Grade: easy-moderate ups and downs, with a descent of 600m/1950ft, and an ascent of 180m/590ft at the end of the walk

Equipment: stout shoes (walking boots preferable), long trousers, windproof, sunhat, fleece, picnic, water

How to get there: 🚌 53, 56 or 78 to Faial or 🚌 56, 103 or 138 to Faial or Santana, then taxi to the Rancho Pico das Pedras on the ER218
To return: 🚌 56, 103 or 138 from Cruzinhas

Short walk: Pico das Pedras — Queimadas — Pico das Pedras. 4km/2.5mi; 1h10min. Easy. Stout lace-up shoes with good grip (the path can be *very* slippery), picnic, water. Access/return: 🚗 car or taxi to/from the Rancho Pico das Pedras on the ER218, where the Levada do Caldeirão Verde crosses the road (Car tour 4). Walk through the 'ranch', with the chalets to your left and the restaurant to the right: the levada continues on the far side of the buildings; follow it to Queimadas and back.

Alternative walk: Queimadas — Caldeirão Verde — Cruzinhas. 23km/14.3mi; 6h30min. Grade, equipment, access: see Walk 22, page 97. Do Walk 22 first. On returning to Queimadas from Caldeirão Verde, follow the levada to the crossing of the ER218 at the Rancho Pico das Pedras. Then do the walk described below. Return on 🚌 56 or 103 from Cruzinhas.

T his walk is at its best in summer or early autumn, when the hydrangeas bordering the levada are bursting with melon-sized blossoms and the tiny terraces in the valleys are aglow with golden hayricks.

Start the walk at the R ANCHO P ICO DAS P EDRAS, 250m/yds below the Pico das Pedras forestry house. The **Levada do Caldeirão Verde** crosses the ER218 here. Follow the blue and yellow sign, heading southeast for 'Faial' (or, for the Short walk, go west towards Queimadas). Stroll beside the levada under the shade of holm oaks, eucalyptus and a 'forest' of cornflower-blue hydrangeas. After **10min** turn left down a track, with the levada beside you on your left. Five minutes later, turn down left again; don't follow the narrow levada

Hydrangeas flank the start of the walk, near the Rancho Pico das Pedras

The steep terracing in the Ribeira Seca near Cruzinhas is at its most colourful in summer.

ahead — the path is too overgrown. In **20min** a track comes in from behind you and to the right: ignore it. Five minutes later, ignore another track off to the right. In **30min** you pass a lone house on the left. Keep ahead downhill for 400m/yds, to a crossroads (**35min**). This is **Cova da Roda**. A track goes left to Santana, and the one we have been descending continues ahead towards Faial, immediately passing a water tank on the left. Turn down *sharp right* here (sign: 'CRUZINHAS').

As you descend, look out left for an old stone-laid trail on the far side of the **Ribeira da Abelheira**, and for the path down to it. (If you miss this path, your track will end at a small tunnel bored for water exploration; just retrace your steps for about 200m/yds to find the path, on your *right*.) You descend to a STONE BRIDGE (**45min**). Ten minutes later you have splendid views of 'Eagle Rock', before dropping down into the Lombo do Galego Valley.

At **Lombo do Galego** (**1h15min**) you meet a road; follow it down to the right (left goes to Faial). The old trail has been preserved where possible; *pale red dots* mark the steps where it leaves the road. Your first turn-off is 600m/yds downhill, on the left (120m above a roadside picnic table, also on the left). Keep watching for the old trail (easily identified by its street lights), if you want to avoid the road. (But the road is so little used, and the beauty of the Ribeira Seca terracing so absorbing, that you may prefer just to follow the road!)

At **Fajã da Murta** you cross the **Ribeira Seca** (**2h05min**), one of the three great rivers flowing to Faial. From here it's a 30-minute climb on the trail; you cross the road once more before reaching **Cruzinhas** and the ER103 (**2h35min**). There is a large BUS SHELTER nearby.

22 QUEIMADAS • LEVADA DO CALDEIRÃO VERDE • SANTANA

Distance: 18km/11.2mi; 5h15min

Grade: moderate, but you must be sure-footed and have a head for heights. The levada path is very slippery and broken away in places. **Danger of vertigo** throughout (very severe drops on one side, adequately protected by fences, *but these often come down in storms*). Four tunnels (10min total). Steep descent to Santana.

Equipment: walking boots, torch, long trousers, fleece, windproof, whistle, picnic, plastic bottle/water purifying tablets, walking stick

How to get there and return: 🚌 56, 103 or 138 or 🚗 to/from Santana, from where you can take a taxi to Queimadas to begin the walk.

Short walks: Levada do Caldeirão Verde. Follow the main walk as long as you like; return the same way. Or follow the levada east to the Rancho Pico das Pedras (Short walk 21 in reverse). Take a picnic and fleece, and *wear lace-up shoes with very good grip; when damp, the red clay soil here is like a skating rink!* Be sure to ask the taxi driver to return for you. 🚗: Travelling by car, see the notes for Car tour 4 on pages 27-28: you may prefer to park at the Rancho Pico das Pedras on the ER218.

Think green. Think of rain forests ... of emeralds. This is Queimadas — a mossy paradise. Take advantage of the 10-minute break in the bus journey at Poiso or Ribeiro Frio and fortify yourself with a warm drink or a 'Madeiran breakfast' (a glass of sweet Madeira wine and a warm hard-boiled egg). This will set you up for the drop in temperature on the descent to the north coast — where as much as 2m/80in of rain can fall in a year!

When you arrive at **Queimadas Park** (*P*22), you will find two charming *pousadas*. **Begin the walk** by passing the lower houses, to discover yet another *pousada* — this one a miniature for the muscovy ducks who live in the pools. Cross the wooden bridge and follow the wide path beside the old

The Levada do Caldeirão Verde (Walks 22, 23 and 28) is densely wooded with heath trees and laurels, creating a lovely play of light and shade. Heath tree branches are used all over Madeira for fencing. Their gnarled curves make a pretty picture, straight out of a story book.

Levada do Caldeirão Verde. The red clay underfoot is *diabolically slippery* — walk on moss where you can. In **13min** pass through a gate, beyond which the path narrows. Four minutes later, be sure to leave the levada where it is broken away — the paths down and back up are slippery too.

The views are spectacular as you follow the levada westwards to one of the most remote parts of the island. After crossing two ravines — the **Ribeira dos Cedros (27min)** and the **Ribeira da Fonte do Louro (45min)** — you come in about **1h** to the first, very short TUNNEL. Two minutes beyond the exit, ignore a path off right signposted to Ilha. *(Walk 28 leaves us here.)* Immediately you plunge into the second tunnel (five minutes). There is a path on the right at this tunnel exit, too; it joins the Ilha path. The third tunnel lies just beyond this path; it's very low: *keep your head down* for the next two minutes. Not far past this third tunnel, you must leave the levada again to avoid an overhanging precipice.

Go through a final, very short tunnel in a couple of minutes and, 13 minutes later (**1h35min**), come to a spillway and a sluice. Climb up the path at the left of the spillway to see the lovely 300m/1000ft-high falls and pool, the **Caldeirão Verde** ('Green Cauldron'). Then continue on the levada. In a few minutes (**1h45min**) you will come to our favourite picnic spot — a promontory in the sun overlooking the **Ribeira Grande**, 500m/1650ft below.

From here allow 3h30min to descend to **Santana** via the Queimadas road. Turn right on the main road; the bus leaves from the TOWN HALL (the building with a clock; **5h15min**).

23 QUEIMADAS • CALDEIRÃO DO INFERNO • QUEIMADAS

Map pages 98-99 **Distance:** 15.5km/9.6mi; just over 5h

Grade: as Walk 22, page 97. But because the section between Caldeirão Verde and Caldeirão do Inferno is *prone to landslides and not protected by fences,* we recommend this walk for experts only.

Equipment: walking boots, long trousers, plastic rainhat, fleece, windproof, raingear, whistle, picnic, plastic bottle/water purifying tablets, torch, walking stick

How to get there and return: 🚗 car or taxi to/from Queimadas (or the Rancho Pico das Pedras: see Short walk 21, page 95). If travelling by bus, see Walk 22, page 97, and add 1h30min to walk down to Santana.

Alternative walk: Queimadas — Caldeirão do Inferno — Pico Ruivo tunnel — Fajã da Nogueira — ER103. 20km/12.4mi; 6h40min. Map continues on reverse of touring map. Grade, equipment, bus or taxi access as main walk. In addition to the hazards of the main walk, you must pass through a tunnel 2.4km/1.5mi long. *Each member of the party must carry a good torch.* Follow the main walk to the Caldeirão do Inferno. Then return to the Pico Ruivo tunnel (20min). Plunge in. You exit about 40min later by booming waterfalls and clear pools, where the Ribeira Seca, coming down from its source on the Pico das Torres, crashes into the levada. Another tunnel (12min to pass) lurks beyond this one. After these, the final few tunnels are a doddle. The levada is soon covered by a jeep track. About 1h30min from entering the Ruivo tunnel take the track down left to the power station (1h; Walk 24b ascends this track). From the power station walk on for 1h15min to the ER103 (🚌 56, 103).

The awe-inspiring chasm of the Caldeirão do Inferno is hidden below the eastern flanks of Pico Canário and the northern escarpment of Ruivo — about as close to the heart of primeval Madeira as you can get. As always, the levada builders have been there before you, taming the wilderness and opening your path.

Water for the Levada dos Tornos is captured at three main sources (described in Walk 24, page 102); the Caldeirão do Inferno is just one of them. Left: crossing the Ribeira Grande, on the approach to the 'Inferno' ('Hell's Cauldron'). Right: at the source. Don't expect to see roaring waterfalls here; this is just surface water, pouring down from Pico Canário (1591m/5220ft). What is magnificent is the escarpment rising 300m/1000ft above you — at its most impressive after rain.

The walk begins at **Queimadas**. Use the notes for Walk 22, page 97, as far as the sunny promontory (**1h45min**). If you picnic here, toss some bread into the air for the aptly named swifts, and watch these acrobatic birds catch it in mid-flight! Then continue along the levada. Another impassable section of levada is encountered in **2h**: slither down to the right and scramble back up again. In **2h05min** come to steps up to the left (the levada takes its source not far ahead, in a beautiful setting with a waterfall). These steps are easily climbed, but coming down it's another story — a descent into nothingness, with no protective fencing.

You ascend 80m/260ft to a newer levada, the **Levada do Pico Ruivo**, at 960m/3150ft (**2h13min**). Two tunnels are seen ahead here. To the left is a short tunnel (no torch needed) opening onto more fine views. The 2.4km/1.5mi-long Pico Ruivo tunnel has old railway tracks dating from its excavation. Steps also continue uphill here (we have been told that they lead to the Pico Ruivo path from Ilha mentioned in Walk 28, but have not had time to investigate). To the right is a large WATER TANK. Skirt the edge of the tank (there is cable fencing). Just beyond the tank you have to walk under a waterfall and will no doubt get soaked. Immediately afterwards, go through a first short TUNNEL. Three more follow. Then you come to roaring waterfalls in a cavern at the head of the **Ribeira Grande** (**2h27min**). This chasm is crossed via two very NARROW BRIDGES (see opposite) or, in dry weather, you can descend to the river bed below. Beyond here you pass through four more short tunnels (the first one *appears* to be blocked off — the opening is just a narrow gap at the right-hand side). You come to the setting shown here — the

Caldeirão do Inferno (**2h32min**), source of the Levada do Pico Ruivo.

Dwarfed by this escarpment lies a tiny levada channel — just a trickle in a grassy sun-trap. It's so still you can almost hear the trees breathing. Relax at this magnificent picnic spot before returning to **Queimadas** (just over **5h**) ... or going on to the nearby valley of Fajã da Nogueira via the Pico Ruivo tunnel (Alternative walk).

Map: reverse of touring map   **Distance:** see Walks a and b below

Grade: both suggestions are easy-moderate, with a climb/descent of 400m/1300ft on tracks. (The initial climb is tedious in the extreme, but you will find it well worth the effort!)

Equipment: stout shoes, long trousers, sunhat, fleece, windproof, picnic, water, torch, walking stick

How to get there and return: 🚗 car or taxi to the power station at Fajã da Nogueira. (Also accessible by 🚌 103 or 138 to the turn-off for the power station on the ER103; add a soul-destroying 4.5km each way.)

Walk a: Pico da Nogueira. 7km/4.4mi; 2h30min. **Walk b: Ribeira Seca.** 11km/6.8mi; 3h40min. These routes diverge at the 40min-point.

Alternative walk: Levada do Pico Ruivo and Levada da Serra. 14km/ 8.7mi; 5h45min. *A more satisfying walk than either a or b above, but only recommended for sure-footed walkers with a head for heights;* ***danger of vertigo.*** At time of writing this path was adequately protected by cable fencing, but it may well come down in storms. Equipment as above, but wear walking boots; take a whistle and plastic bottle/water purifying tablets. Follow Walk b to the Ribeira Seca and back. Continue *past* the track you ascended. Walk with the flow of the Levada do Pico Ruivo (and later the Levada da Serra) for 1h25min, until you come to a tunnel (4h). Just inside it is the underground water tank (it was not possible to build this large reservoir on the open mountainside). Descend the track in front of the tunnel and, less than 10min downhill (just before a keepers' house), turn right uphill to a T-junction. You reach the top of the pipe on Pico da Nogueira, outside the tank (35min from the tunnel). To return to the power station, go down the track and, at the fork before the keepers' house, continue down the main track. In 15min (5h) ford the Ribeira da Fajã da Nogueira (or cross it on a makeshift bridge). You meet your outgoing track 10min later, just above the clearing with the enormous *til* trees. The power station is 35min downhill.

The Levada dos Tornos (Walk 7) was born here in the wilderness of Fajã da Nogueira in 1971, when the power station was inaugurated. Water for the Tornos is captured at three main sources. One lies far to the northwest: an extremely long tunnel carries water from the Porco and São Jorge rivers directly to this power station. Another conduit is

the rebuilt Levada da Serra do Faial e Juncal, which runs from the Juncal River to an underground reservoir and then a pipe on Pico da Nogueira. The third source is the Caldeirão do Inferno (Walk 23): its waters flow through the Pico Ruivo tunnel to the same pipe, whence both levadas plummet down to the power station.

All the walks begin at **Fajã da Nogueira**. Climb the jeep track at the right of the POWER STATION. In **20min** you have superb views of the Torres ahead and Pico da Nogueira, with its pipe, on your left. In **35min** Pico do Arieiro is just ahead; the Miradouro do Juncal is also prominent. Pass a clearing at the **Montado do Sabugal**, with two enormous fire-ravaged *til* trees. (During this walk you will see some of the oldest laurels on the island, with trunks over 8ft in diameter.) Two minutes past the clearing (**40min**), a track joins from the left.

Walk a turns left down this track, in 10 minutes fording the **Ribeira da Fajã da Nogueira** (or crossing on a makeshift bridge). Continue uphill for about 20 minutes, to a fork near the keepers' house, where you ignore the track to the right. In **1h20min** you come to the top of the pipe, outside the underground reservoir. Nearby is a grassy verge, perfect for picnicking. From here you overlook the sinuous Ribeira do Juncal and the Metade Valley. You're at 960m/3150ft; not far below, you can see an old levada that used to run between Balcões and Fajã da Nogueira, now completely crumbled away. Return the same way (**2h30min**); from the keepers' house, you could take a detour up left (20min return) to see the levada and underground reservoir.

Walk b keeps ahead, climbing to the **Levada do Pico Ruivo** (covered by a track; **1h10min**). Turn right, walking against the water's flow and coming to the setting shown below left. Past two keepers' houses and some short tunnels, at **1h40min** you enter a TUNNEL WITH RAILWAY TRACKS (12 minutes). You'll hear the roar of waterfalls on the far side before you exit by crashing falls and clear pools, high up in the **Ribeira Seca** (**1h 52min**). From this superb picnic spot the PICO RUIVO TUNNEL leads to Walk 23, but we turn back to the POWER STATION (**3h40min**).

Left, Walk b: At 1h10min the Cabeço da Fajã dos Vinháticos is just in front of you; its velvety emerald ridges ripple down the north side of the Ribeira Seca. Right: The Alternative walk edges the Levada da Serra between the two tracks. Better fencing was built in the late 1990s.

25 LEVADA DO FURADO: RIBEIRO FRIO •
LAMACEIROS • PORTELA

See also photograph page 2   **Distance:** 11km/6.8mi; 3h25min

Grade: moderate, but you must be sure-footed and have a head for heights (**danger of vertigo**). The most precipitous sections of the levada are well protected with iron railings, *but there are several exposed stretches without fencing.*

Equipment: walking boots or stout shoes that grip on slippery surfaces, long trousers, windproof, sunhat, fleece, plastic bottle/water purifying tablets, picnic, whistle

How to get there: 🚌 56, 103 or 138 to Ribeiro Frio
To return: 🚌 53 or 78 from Portela

Short walk: Ribeiro Frio — Balcões — Ribeiro Frio. 2km/1.3mi; 40min. Easy; 🚌 56, 103 or 138 or 🚗 to/from Ribeiro Frio. The signposted path is below the souvenir shop. Follow it beside the dry levada; in 20 minutes you'll pass through a cut in the towering, moss-covered basalt and find yourself high in the Metade Valley. At a fork, where the old levada goes left; turn right and you're at the Balcões (*P*25) in a minute. Superb views (see photograph page 28); snack bar en route.

Alternative walks: grade, equipment, access as main walk

1 Ribeiro Frio — Ribeira do Poço do Bezerro — Chão das Feiteiras — Ribeiro Frio. 7km/4.3mi; 2h50min. Ascent of 300m/1000ft; equipment as main walk; *map inset opposite*. A five-star walk, *but not suitable in heavy mist!* 🚌 or 🚗 to/from Ribeiro Frio. Follow the main walk to the 1h-point, then clamber 2m/6ft up to the path on the bank above the left-hand levada channel. Follow this narrow levada to its source in the Ribeira do Poço do Bezerro (2h; lovely pools). Retrace your steps for 30m/yds, then turn left up a narrow path. This takes you up to a plateau (the Chão das Feiteiras; 2h15min). Head straight across northeast through ferns *(feiteiras)* towards three farm buildings (in mist, you won't see them until you reach them in 10min). Turn right on the grassy track in front of them but, after 200m/yds, turn left on a grassy trail, going through a gate in 20m/yds. Soon cobbles come underfoot. Descend to the ER103, cross it, and pick up the continuing trail 200m/yds downhill. This beautiful old trail emerges just above the trout hatchery (2h50min).

2 Ribeiro Frio — Lamaceiros — Levada da Serra. You can join the Levada da Serra at the Lamaceiros waterhouse and continue for as long as you like: see Walk 10, page 70.

3 Ribeiro Frio — Pico do Suna — Portela. 13.5km/8.4mi; 4h20min. Follow the main walk for 2h10min. Just before the tunnel, take the path on the left; fork right to climb above the tunnel, then keep straight uphill. When you meet a crossing trail, turn left up to the fire tower at Pico do Suna (30min). Return the same way and continue to Portela.

T his is a walk to which we return again and again, to enjoy the wonderful play of light and shade along the levada, the frisson of excitement at the Cabeço Furado, and the spectacular views in the second half of the walk.
   Begin the walk just below the bar/restaurant at **Ribeiro Frio**. Here you will see a SIGNPOST TO PORTELA on your right (further downhill, on the left, is the sign for Balcões; *P*25). Here you join the fast-flowing **Levada do Furado**. In **20min** pass a tunnel on the right, with a waterfall. In **1h**, just by a bridge over the **Ribeira do Poço do Bezerro,** two fast-flowing

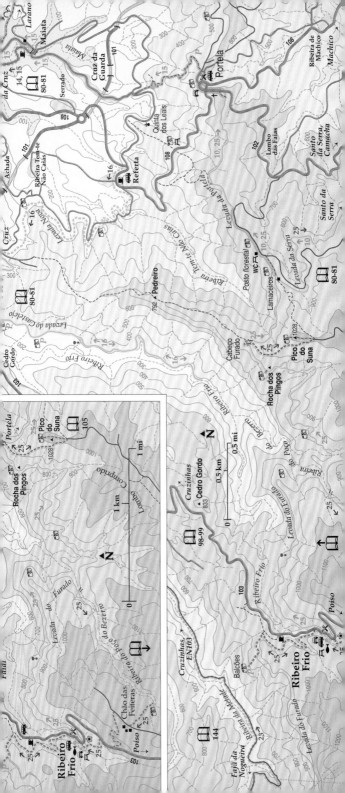

Anyone can follow the levada for just a short way, to revel in the play of light and shade over rocks and water-falls, laurel and heath trees. The second part of the walk, beyond the Lamaceiros waterhouse, is com-pletely different. You cross sunny pastures, enjoying panoramas of majestic mountains, proud valleys, and the tranquillity of the north coast villages in the distance.

levadas course down into the main channel at a grassy verge *(where Alternative walk 1 climbs the embankment).* The finches here have been tamed by 'Landscapers' (see photo-graph on page 2), and will expect to be fed some titbits! About eight minutes beyond this bridge **keep careful watch** for the first of many deviations: it is easier **and safer** to cross the shal-low stream beds than follow the levada.

In **1h20min** you pass through a massive cleft in the rock, where stepping stones bridge the channel. Soon there are splendid views left to the high peaks. At **2h** a strong path off to the left leads to a fine view over São Roque and Faial after only a minute. At about **2h10min** you will pass through a very short tunnel. Just before it, a path on the left doubles back over the levada and climbs to Pico do Suna *(Alternative walk 3).* Two minutes later you come to a precipice, where the very narrow levada path is cut into the Suna escarpment at the **Cabeço Furado**. This excitement lasts for 10 minutes.

By **2h35min** you'll reach the peaceful setting of the **Lama-ceiros** waterhouse and look out east to São Lourenço. *(From here you can go on to the Levada da Serra; Alternative walk 2; there is also another path up to Pico do Suna.)* About 30m/yds past the waterhouse, turn left down a path to find the narrow **Levada da Portela**. Follow it to a forestry house (pic-nic tables, toilets), and here join a track at the right. Descend gently, with marvellous views of Faial, Penha de Águia and Porto da Cruz. When the levada 'disappears', stay on the track. After 250m/yds, go left on a clearly marked path, to find the levada on your left and pastures on your right. At a fork, head right, following the levada (now on your right). You'll come to a derelict waterhouse. Go left here: slippery earthen steps take you down to the ER102. Walk 150m left downhill, pass the 'Portela' sign, then turn left on the *Machico* road to the bar 'Portela a Vista' (**3h25min**); the bus stop is opposite.

26 CIRCUIT AROUND SANTANA

See map pages 98-99   **Distance:** 9.5km/5.9mi; 2h55min

Grade: moderate, with ascents/descents of about 200m/650ft overall. You must be sure-footed, but there is no danger of vertigo.

Equipment: stout shoes (walking boots preferable), sunhat, picnic, water

How to get there and return: 🚌 56, 103 or 138 to/from Cortado (just east of Santana) or 🚗: park at Cortado, near the two 'Santana' houses

Short walks

1 **Pico da Boneca.** 3km/2mi; 50min. Easy. Access as main walk. Follow the main walk to the 50min-point, but continue back to Cortado.

2 **Levada do Cantinho.** 4.5km/2.8mi; 1h30min. Grade as main walk. Access: 🚌 56, 103 or 138 or 🚗 to/from the chapel at Santo António. Walk down the road opposite the front of the chapel, picking up the main walk at just past the 1h05min-point. Follow it to the 2h35min-point, then turn left along the road for 320m/yds, back to the chapel.

This gentle ramble round Santana takes you through lovely agricultural landscapes and opens up a wealth of coastal and inland views. And if you find the walk too 'tame', then interrupt it halfway along: take a 40 minute return detour to the cable car station, and enjoy the exhilarating ride down to Fajã da Rocha do Navio (Wed/Sat/Sun *only*)!

Start out at **Cortado**. Follow the level road to the left (sign: 'PICO DA BONECA, MIRADOURO'). Ignore a road down left (after 120m), then a tunnel on the right (after 250m).* In **12min**, at a Y-fork, ignore the track up right to the antennas (you will return that way); keep ahead.** Some 300m/yds further on, climb a good zigzag path on the right to the trig point on **Pico da Boneca (25min)**. Before you is the whole spread of Santana in the west and Faial in the east. Disappointly, the high peaks behind Santana are *not* impressive from this perspective.

Leaving the peak, start down the path you ascended but, at a fork, keep left on a contouring path along the east side of the ridge, with fabulous views down over Faial and Eagle Rock, as well as the 'prow'-shaped rock of the Rocha do Navio. When the path comes to a pass below the antennas, turn right on a track. Follow this downhill to the junction encountered earlier, turn left and retrace your outgoing route.

Just 120m/yds short of Cortado, turn right down the road passed earlier (**50min**; it *should* be signposted to Santana). At a fork almost immediately, go right. Eventually an old cobbled trail comes underfoot; it takes you down across the Santo António River and up to the road in **Santo António**, opposite a bar (**1h05min**). Note the cobbled trail at the left

---

*You could go through this short tunnel and follow a narrow levada on the east side of the ridge; the path is very narrow and unstable in places.
**After 150m/yds you pass a wide path down left. It is an alternative to the route we use, but is very steep and overgrown (although it is the *only* council-maintained path into the valley). If you take this, when you reach a levada, turn left, then take the path half-right almost immediately and pick up the main walk at just after the 1h05min-point.

of the bar: it is your return route from Santana. Turn right and walk 320m/ yds to a small chapel on the right, then go left on the road opposite. Follow this downhill towards a large house with a well-landscaped garden with a large green metal bird cage.

Just *before* the house, take the *very narrow,* overgrown path at the right of a concrete shed (**1h10min**). Zigzag downhill, cross a footbridge in two minutes, and arrive at the **Levada do Cantinho**. Turn right on the very slippery clay path through thickets of sugar cane, and follow the levada, ignoring all turn-offs. But some 20 minutes along *do* turn right briefly — to a railed viewpoint by a goods cableway, from where you enjoy the splendid view shown below (perhaps even see the passenger cable car in flight!). Then continue on the levada, rounding the promontory below Covas. At a fork, where another levada runs straight ahead, go right.

When you meet a road in **Parlatorio** (**1h55min**), turn left. (Or first detour 1km to the right, down to the cable car station, referring to the map on page 88.) Follow this road uphill to the church in **Santana** (**2h05min**). Pass to the right of the church, then turn left and left again on asphalt. Ignore a road off left and cross straight over another road ('Tia Clementia' may be signposted off to the left here). Walk to the left of the school, descend across a stream and, as the road curves right uphill, take the cobbled trail on the left — below a high arch, near overhead electricity wires. This trail brings you back to the road in **Santo António**, by the bar (**2h35min**). Now retrace your steps back up to **Cortado** (**2h55min**).

View down over Fajã da Rocha do Navio from the Levada do Cantinho

27 TWO WALKS FROM BOAVENTURA

See photograph page 29   Distance, grade: see walks a and b below

Equipment: walking boots, sunhat, water, picnic, walking stick; extra fleece and windproof in cool weather, optional swimwear in summer

How to get there and return: 🚐 6 or 132 🚗 to/from Boaventura

Walk a: Levada de Cima. 9.5km/6mi; 3h10min. Easy-moderate ups and downs of 170m/560ft overall, but you must be agile and have a head for heights (awkward descent at Roçada; **danger of vertigo** on the levada)

Walk b: Boaventura — Arco de São Jorge. 3.3km/2mi; 1h20min. Quite easy ascent of 180m/600ft. 🚐 6, 103 or 132 to return. (Or do as a descent from Arco.) Motorists can shorten the route by 3km/45min by parking at the Caminho do Calhau (see map).

To link both walks, see dashed green line on the map; allow 45min.

T wo of the most delightful walks on the island! Walk a is a flower-filled hike through cultivation alternating with a jungle-like wilderness; it takes you across rock pools where you can bathe, and finally along an ancient free-form levada. At the end of the walk, as you descend to Boaventura, you look out beyond the palm-shaded cemetery towards an old zigzag trail clinging precariously to a sugar-loaf cliff. It looks impossibly vertiginous, but it's easy! Walk b takes you there.

Both walks begin at the CHURCH in **Boaventura**, from where you walk southeast along the ER101 towards Santana.

Walk a departs just past the church: climb the concrete steps on the right, opposite the telephone kiosk (sign: 'ORIGEM LEVADA'). In one minute fork left up more steps. You follow electricity wires up a ridge, through a tight cluster of houses abounding with flowers. After passing a water tap on the right (**12min**), the way levels out amidst a profusion of sunflowers and vines, and the concrete runs out. Keep ahead on the path. At a Y-fork keep left, ignoring the right turn to a concrete building. You pass to the right of an old stone house. The path rises, widens to a trail, and forks (**25min**). Ignore the left turn ('Levada'); keep ahead towards 'ROÇADA', dipping and rising as you cross various tributaries of the Ribeira dos Moinhos. Ignore paths down to the right.

A walking stick is helpful on the steep descent to the **Ribeira dos Moinhos** at Roçada (**48min**). Just *before* the trail (or new road) crosses the river, turn left on a narrow path, to cross the river on a bridge. On the far side, turn left on a wide path in a grassy setting. By some river pools you cross back over to the other side of the river and follow a good stone-laid path. In **1h03min**, *before* the terraces on the far side of the valley give way to trees, take the narrow path on the right (signposted 'POÇO SALÃO') down to the river pools (the way ahead goes to Falca). Beyond the pools, your ongoing path lies slightly to the right. At a fork a minute uphill, climb steeply to the left. In three minutes you come to the **Levada de Cima**. Its source (*madre*) is less than five minutes to the left.

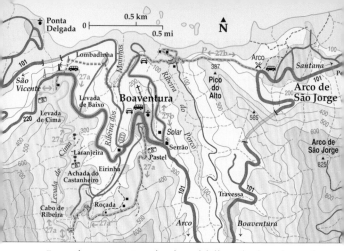

From the source, turn back and follow the levada north, passing some paths down to the right. Like many old levadas, this one is not always corseted in concrete; it flows quickly and freely — sometimes shallow, sometimes deep … through cultivation, under chestnuts, below dramatic cliffs. A couple of short stretches at river crossings are quite vertiginous. Eventually you pass the first house of **Levada de Cima** (**1h 55min**). In **2h03min** concrete steps at the far side of a lone house descend to a microwave station on the main road. Press on: in a minute you enjoy fine views west — as far as Ribeira da Janela. Five minutes later the levada drops over the cliff and into a tank; from here you overlook Ponta Delgada. Return to the concrete steps above the microwave station and descend to the road (bus 6 and 132). If no bus is due, follow the road back to **Boaventura** (**3h**) — a beautiful stroll, looking out towards the setting for Walk b.

For **Walk b**, continue along the road for 300m, then turn left in front of the electricity substation, passing the Solar (hotel) on your left. Some 1.2km down this road, descend the path on the right, the 'Camino do Calhau' (**20min**). After crossing the **Ribeira do Porco** on a stone bridge, it's worth exploring the picturesque old ruins to the left, above the mouth of the river — either take the narrow path on the left through a red clay gully (an awkward scramble at the outset) or bear right on the main path and, at a fork by a stone ruin, turn left. We *think* these are the remains of an old textile mill: our Madeiran history book refers to such ruins in this area, where 'fabric was made using the red clay obtained nearby'.

From the lone ruin the beautiful old trail (Caminho da Entrosa) rises in easy zigzags up the vertical cliff. The views straight down to the sea are breathtaking, but sturdy railings ensure no danger. Historians marvelled at the huge house leeks on these cliffs ('the size of hats'). The trail emerges at the Snack Bar Arco on the ER101 (**1h20min**; bus 6, 103, 132).

28 QUEIMADAS • VALE DA LAPA • ILHA DE SÃO JORGE

Map pages 98-99; photographs pages 39 (left) and 97

Distance: 8.5km/5.3mi; 3h15min

Grade: moderate-strenuous, with a descent of 550m/1800ft on a very steep and slippery path; you must be sure-footed, and this walk is not recommended after heavy rain. Red and yellow waymarking.

Equipment: walking boots, long trousers, sunhat, fleece, windproof, picnic, plastic bottle/water purifying tablets, walking stick

How to get there: 🚌 56, 103 or 138 to Santana, then taxi to Queimadas
To return: 🚌 103 from Ilha de São Jorge

Alternative walk: Queimadas — Vale da Lapa — Queimadas. 10km/6.2mi; 3h05min. Quite easy. Access/return: 🚗 car or taxi to/from Queimadas (or the Rancho Pico das Pedras: see Short walk 21, page 95). Follow the main walk to the 1h25min-point, visit the tiny forestry house, then return the same way.

Two walks in one: on this excursion you enjoy the shady meanderings of the Levada do Caldeirão Verde, and then you leave it for the sunny heights above São Jorge, with views of the north coast villages round to Santana.

Begin at **Queimadas**: follow WALK 22 for **1h**, when you pass through a very short tunnel (you won't need a torch). Two minutes beyond the tunnel exit, take the path off right (signposted 'Vale da Lapa'). In 20m/yds ignore the path sharp left signposted to Pico Ruivo and continue ahead (signposted 'Ilha'). The path is now waymarked with red and yellow flashes all the way to your destination. You walk along what was once a beautiful stone-edged levada planted with hydrangeas, but the channel has since been filled in with soil. You have fine views to the right over the Levada do Caldeirão Verde and a lower levada in the same valley — the **Ribeira dos Arcos**.

In 20 minutes there is a signposted short detour left to a 'Fonte' (spring). You then reach a GATE (**1h25min**), just beyond which a path comes in sharply from the left — from the **Vale da Lapa** forestry house. (Allow an extra 15 minutes return if you want to make a detour to this isolated *posto floretal*, a delightful place for a picnic.) The main walk keeps ahead here, descending a very steep and slippery jungle-like stream bed.

When you meet a track at a T-junction (20 minutes from the gate; **1h45min**), follow it downhill. At a bend to the right, leave the track and walk ahead past a signpost pointing back to Pico Ruivo. Descending in a gully, cross a track and follow the sign for 'Ilha'. Always keep ahead over ensuing track crossings. When you come to a fork, ignore the right turn to 'Lombada do Meio'; head left for 'Granel' (the lower part of Ilha, near the church, but usually spelled 'Garnal'). The BUS STOP is by the church and bar in **Ilha (3h)**.

29 LEVADA DA FAJÃ DO RODRIGUES

Photograph page 19 **Distance:** 7km/4.3mi; 2h25min

Grade: easy, level walking, but the levada path can be slippery

Equipment: stout lace-up shoes, sunhat, *torch*

How to get there and return: 🚌 to/from the levada: take the ER208 from Feiteiras (signs: 'Ginjas, Lanço, Parque Empresarial de São Vicente'; Car tours 1, 5). Keep following 'Parque Empresarial de São Vicente', going left at two T-junctions (0.9km, 2.4km). At 3.5km you pass this large industrial estate, on the left. Continue uphill for another 400m and park near a water purification plant; the levada is just above the large tank.

The Fajã do Rodrigues Levada used to be too dangerous to follow very far upstream, but since its upgrading in 2001 everyone can now explore this beautiful wilderness, abounding with ancient laurels, ferns and birdsong.

Start out at the WATER TREATMENT PLANT on the ER208. Walk a short way uphill, join the **Levada da Fajã do Rodrigues** and turn right. You come to a huge SLUICE, where water from a 1.5km-long tunnel bored into the rock on the left pours into the levada (**4min**) — a tremendously invigorating spot!

Threading your way below eucalyptus and beside a plethora of vegetation, you penetrate a deep valley, where the laurel-coated pinnacles of the **Furna da Areia** tower above you. A good pumice path has come under foot, flanked by steel railings. Twenty minutes from the sluice you reach a *caldeirão* (**24min**), a high rock basin where a narrow waterfall drops almost 200m/650ft (if it hasn't been such a dry year that it's dried up!). You won't get *too* wet splashing below it, and it's worth continuing along the levada *through* the first short tunnel (torch required; **35min**). (The levada takes its source 2km northwest in the Ribeira do Inferno; much of it flows through tunnels.)

Return the same way, catching glimpses down left of the lovely view shown on page 19. From the SLUICE (**1h**) continue southeast along the beautifully planted levada, past a few cottages with vegetable plots and tired apple orchards. Eventually you pass two well-placed picnic tables on sunny promontories, before reaching a TUNNEL in the **Ribeira da Vargem** (**1h45min**; *not shown on our map*), from where this levada flows over 3km to the power station at Serra de Água.

From here return the same way to the ER208 and the WATER TREATMENT PLANT (**2h25min**).

30 LOMBADA DA PONTA DO SOL •
LEVADA NOVA • TABUA • RIBEIRA BRAVA

Map pages 114-115; photograph page 34

Distance: 15km/9.3mi; 3h50min

Grade: moderate-strenuous, with an overall ascent of 200m/650ft and a steep descent of 400m/1300ft at the end of the walk. You must be sure-footed and have a head for heights (**danger of vertigo** on the levada).

Equipment: stout shoes or walking boots, long trousers, sunhat, picnic, water, walking stick; extra fleece and windproof in cool weather

How to get there: 🚌 142 to Formiga (Fohr-**mee**-gah; it means 'ant'!) on the ER222, 2.1km east of the turn-off to Ponta do Sol
To return: 🚌 any suitable bus from Ribeira Brava

Alternative walk: Lombada's levadas. Distance optional; equipment as above *(plus torch)*. Access: 🚌 as above or 🚗 to/from Lombada. Two levadas take their source high on the eastern flanks of the Ribeira da Ponta do Sol; *both are vertiginous, the old one **extremely** so.* You could explore the old Levada do Moinho for a short time (see text below), then return and follow the main walk to the Levada Nova. Pursue this new levada *to the left,* up the valley, for as long as you like, then return and follow the main walk — perhaps to the Ribeira da Caixa and back.

The enormous rose-pink *solar* at Lombada was for centuries the largest country house on Madeira. And it stood in the largest private estate — the Lombada dos Esmeraldos, stretching from the Paúl da Serra down to the sea between the Ponta do Sol and Caixa valleys. This huge domain had been given by Zarco to one of his sons, who cultivated sugar cane with great success. It was later bought by João de Esmeraldo, a friend of Christopher Columbus. At one time 80 slaves worked in Esmeraldo's plantations and mills; with the wealth created, he built the mansion and nearby church of the Espírito Santo. There is little evidence of the sugar plantations today, but the valleys are still a tapestry of cultivation.

Start out at **Formiga**: climb the road to **Lombada** (see map; **20min**). Look at the old *solar,* then enjoy the superb view over the **Ribeira da Ponta do Sol** (photograph page 34) from the balcony walkway behind the church. Here an iron gate leads to the old (1400s, but recently repaired) **Levada do Moinho**; it powered the mills in the sugar plantations. To reach the new levada, start back out of Lombada the way you came in, pass the small shop/bar, then take the first left turn. Follow this road quite steeply uphill to a T-junction with another road, where you turn right alongside the **Levada Nova** (**35min**). *(But for the Alternative walk, turn left).*

Now begin to pace out Esmeraldo's domain. Five minutes along, weave between the houses of **Jangão**, then descend steps to a very narrow road, with a building opposite. Go straight over this road, following another road just to the right of the building (a shop). Walk past all the houses below this road; then, after 150m/yds (after the fifth lamp post), by a gap in the roadside retaining wall, descend concrete steps back to the levada (you reach it by a fig tree and shed). In winter and spring calla lilies and yellow-blooming vetch are a perfect foil for the dark rods of sugar cane still cultivated here (probably for the spirit, *aguardente*).

After crossing a concrete path you come into the **Ribeira da Caixa**, soon passing through a very short tunnel. The cane peters out as you leave Esmeraldo's ridge, to be replaced by willow, the odd banana grove, and all the ingredients for a hearty vegetable soup. The lime-green grass here is *so* inviting for a picnic. Ten minutes after passing through the tunnel you come to the head of the valley, where you have to round a narrow path above a small gorge ... while passing below an icy waterfall! There is no way round this obstacle. In hot weather it's a lot of fun, but the path is slippery and *potentially hazardous; go slowly.*

Ten minutes later (**1h15min**) you leave the valley, coming to a road. Cross over and continue on the levada. Only a minute later a concrete track crosses the levada; follow this track 20m/yds downhill to the right, then rejoin the channel (with street lights) on the left. Now head north into the **Ribeira da Tabua**, graced with white iris, broom and sugar cane in spring, hayricks, sweet chestnuts and blackberries in autumn. Beyond a sugar cane grove, in inland **Tabua**, you cross a bridge and then ford a spillway (**2h05min**; or cross a bridge 20m/yds upstream). Heading southeast, then cross the village road on steps. After passing through a cut in the basalt cliffs (**2h15min**), where stepping stones bridge the levada, you enjoy the best views of this valley — its river pools, poplars and hayricks. But along here the path is very vertiginous.

A short tunnel (**2h20min**) takes you into a new valley, and beyond a road, you pass a grassy knoll on the right overlooking coastal Tabua. In under **2h45min** the levada disappears beneath a walkway. Turn left up concrete steps, to **Corujeira** (there is a bar here), where a road descends to the ER222. Follow the road downhill to the right for 50m/yds, to where the levada continues on a high parapet. This is so vertiginous that it is easier to walk down the road: keep left at the junction quickly encountered. Just past the junction, the road makes a U-bend in the **Ribeira da Caldeira**. Here take the *second* set of steps on your right, to descend to the levada. You meet a narrow concrete road (**3h**): turn right and join Walk 31 just after its 4h35min-point, dropping steeply to **Ribeira Brava** (**3h50min**). The BUS STOP is on the seafront esplanade.

31 ENCUMEADA • LEVADA DO LOMBO DO MOURO • RIBEIRA BRAVA

Map begins on the reverse of the touring map and ends below

Distance: 15.5km/9.6mi; 5h25min

Grade: strenuous, with a climb of 300m/985ft to start (but see 'How to get there' below) and a very steep descent of 1300m/4265ft. You must be sure-footed; part of the route can be *very* overgrown.

Equipment: walking boots, long sleeves/trousers, sunhat, fleece, windproof, picnic, plastic bottle/water purifying tablets, whistle, walking stick

How to get there: 🚌 6 or 139 to Encumeada Pass (*not* the Residencial Encumeada), or 🚕 taxi from Ribeira Brava or São Vicente to the Lombo do Mouro signpost on the ER110 (deduct just over 4km/1h30min).
To return: 🚌 any suitable bus from Ribeira Brava

The Lombo do Mouro, a dinosaur's back of a ridge, is the setting for a delightful levada walk … but save it until you've acquired your 'Madeira knees' — the descent to Ribeira Brava will leave them quaking!

Start out at **Encumeada:** walk to the north side of the pass and climb the ER110 to the **Lombo do Mouro** signpost, on your left after just over 4km (**1h30min**). Take the steps at the

The descent to Ribeira Brava (left); the rushing levada and the Lombo do Mouro house, below the escarpment of the Paúl da Serra (Picnic 31)

left of the sign, or follow the tarred spur to its end and take steps from there. *(Don't try to scramble down by the cable hoist!)* Once down at this beautifully sited government rest house and hunting lodge (**1h40min**; **P**31), you join the **Levada do Lombo do Mouro**. Follow its flow, with fine views east towards Pico Grande (Walk 4), Achada da Pinta (Walk 5) and the Arieiro/Ruivo route (Walk 19). Go through a gate in **2h10min** and then perhaps take a break in the tall golden grass, with orange butterflies pursuing the purple thistles and foxgloves, and the levada surging down beside you. Put on protective clothing: the next stretch may be very overgrown!

In **2h40min** you come into the eucalyptus zone, so you know that you have already dropped to below 900m/3000ft. Five minutes later the levada describes a wide arc and descends very steeply (photograph above). In the east the pine forest at Boa Morte (Walk 6) makes a pleasant picture.

From time to time you will be aware of a track sidling up to the levada and eventually you're forced to join it. It takes you to a road (**3h55min**). Turn left for 250m/yds, then go right, down a steep concrete track. When you join another road, follow it downhill for 400m/yds, then go left on concrete. From here on, always take the steepest route downhill, with the dramatic **Brava Valley** close by on your left. At **4h35min** cross straight over another asphalt road; 60m/yds further down, Walk 30 comes in from the right, just in front of a garage. Beyond a stretch of concrete steps, turn left at a T-junction (**4h45min**). At another T-junction (**4h55min**), keep left down more concrete steps. When you meet the ER222, go left downhill and find the final flight of steps down into **Ribeira Brava** (**5h25min**) — where you can collapse in a café. The BUS STOP is on the seafront esplanade.

32 FOLHADAL AND THE NORTE AND RABAÇAS LEVADAS

Map on reverse of touring map   **Distance:** 8.5km/5.3mi; 2h50min

Grade: easy, but you must be sure-footed and have a head for heights (**danger of vertigo** on the Levada das Rabaças). Two tunnels (one fairly long).

Equipment: stout shoes, good torch *for each member of the party*, sunhat, plastic bottle/water purifying tablets, picnic, fleece, windproof

How to get there and return: 🚌 6 or 139 to Encumeada *pass* (*not* the Residencial Encumeada); 🚌 6 to return. Or by 🚗: park at the viewpoint on the north side of the pass (Car tours 1 and 5).

Short walk: Encumeada — Folhadal — Encumeada. 4km/2.5mi; 1h. Equipment, access/return as above. Follow the main walk to Folhadal and back. *A 5-star walk on a fine day; the paths are amply wide, and there is little danger of vertigo, but good torches are essential.*

Alternative walk: Encumeada — Cascalho — Encumeada. 16.5km/ 10.2mi; 5h. *Expert:* very narrow levada paths, many of them unprotected (**danger of vertigo**); at least two potentially hazardous screes; one very long tunnel (often with short patches of thigh-high water at either end). Access/return, equipment as above (but wear walking boots and long trousers and take a whistle). This is an alternative approach to the *caldeirão* (rock basin pouring with waterfalls) visited in Walk 36. Follow the main walk for 2h, then go through the long tunnel (30min). Follow the levada into the Ponta do Sol Valley. Cascalho ('scree') is the source of the Rabaças Levada (3h; see notes page 126). Return the same way.

Power and majesty. These may be your first impressions when you step onto the levada at Encumeada Pass. You are at the centre of the deep north/south cleft that splits the island. The high peaks rise in the east; the magnificent valley of Serra de Água lies to the south. And at your feet, the Levada do Norte, 1.5m/5ft deep and just as wide, surges along in a massive concrete channel. You're bound for Folhadal, a primeval wonderland of ferns and ancient laurels.

Left (top and bottom): greenery on the Levada do Norte path to Folhadal. Right: looking east towards Pico Grande from the Levada das Rabaças, just past the tunnel, where the Levada do Norte comes in from Folhadal. (The fog is pouring out of the tunnel!)

Start the walk opposite the bar/restaurant, on the south side of the pass at **Encumeada**, where a sign indicates 'Folhadal'. Climb concrete steps here up to the **Levada do Norte** and follow it westwards, past the keepers' flower-filled house. You'll be amazed by the abundance of vegetation: conifers of every description, heath and hawthorn, with a tangle of laurel, azaleas, lilies, hydrangeas, and myriad wild flowers. If you're walking here in June, you'll see the splendid cornflower-blue 'Pride of Madeira' in all its glory. In **12min** you come to the promontory of **Lapa do Galho** (**P**32): from here you enjoy fine views down over the valley and the south coast. You can also see the levada continuing to the east and emptying into the metal pipe down to the power station (inaugurated in 1953). There are 50km/31mi of channels north of here (including 11km/ 6.8mi of tunnels). From the power station the water flows on in another 35km/22mi of channels (7km/4.5mi of tunnels) to irrigate the terraces of Ribeira Brava and Câmara de Lobos (see Walk 6).

Past the promontory the levada forks (**14min**). Turn right and follow the Levada do Norte into the tunnel, which will take about 10-12 minutes to pass through. We'll never forget our first walk here: we approached the tunnel to find what looked like a washing machine gone mad. Thick white 'foam' was pouring out of it (see photograph on the previous page) — fog, rushing through from the other side!

The tunnel exit (**25min**) frames your first glimpse of **Folhadal**, a 'museum' of ferns and indigenous trees — *vinháticos, til* trees (laurels) and white-barked *paus brancos* (olive family). But your eyes will be drawn to the *folhados* for which this wood is named — the summer-flowering lily-of-the-valley trees, native only to Madeira. Keep ahead through the *laurisilva*, enjoying views to the São Vicente valley — until you come to a second tunnel (**45min**). From here return* the same way to the levada fork (**1h15min**).

Now turn right to follow the narrower **Levada das Rabaças** (1970), a 'tributary' of the Levada do Norte. It is flowing in from Cascalho, the waterfall basin explored in Walk 36 (and the Alternative walk). In **1h45min** a waterfall on the right heralds a short tunnel (3min to pass). Seven minutes later, you reach a lonely keepers' house above the Pousada dos Vinháticos. In **2h** you come to the long tunnel to Cascalho (*Alternative walk*). Turn back to the 'Folhadal' sign at **Encumeada** (**2h50min**), where the bus stops.

---

*Or first follow the extremely vertiginous levada (no protective fencing) through this and two more tunnels, to a pretty waterhouse on the ER208; allow 2h return (50min in tunnels); see purple arrows on the map.

Map on reverse of touring map; see also photograph page 19

Distance: 6.5km/4mi; 2h05min

Grade: easy-moderate, with a descent/re-ascent of about 150m/500ft. You must be sure-footed and have a head for heights to get all the way to Pináculo (*the levada just before 'the Pinnacle' may be **impassable** in winter, when waterfalls inundate the vertiginous, unprotected path*).

Equipment: walking boots, long trousers, sunhat, fleece, windproof, picnic, plastic bottle/water purifying tablets, whistle

How to get there and return: 🚌 to/from Bica da Cana (Car tour 5)

Alternative walk: ER110 — Pináculo — Bica da Cana. 5km/3mi; 1h45min. Moderate-strenuous ascent of 400m/1300ft; *not always passable in winter, when the path beyond Pináculo may be inundated by waterfalls and **too dangerous to follow***. 🚌 Ask friends to drop you on the ER110, 3.3km uphill from Encumeada, where the road crosses the Levada do Lombo do Mouro. Arrange to be collected later by the white and red pillars at the entrance to the Bica da Cana government refuge. From the ER110 climb steps and follow the Levada do Lombo do Mouro to the right. Beyond its source, a zigzag path takes you up to the Levada da Serra. Turn right; you will reach Pináculo in 1h. Continue on the levada, *past* signposts for Bica da Cana and Caramujo, and then the levada's source. Under 35min from Pináculo, watch for a blue 'hat' painted on a rock on the ground; here climb a path up to Bica da Cana.

O ne of our all-time favourite walks, absolutely gorgeous in its own right … and affording a splendid outlook towards the high peaks. You're just on the eastern flanks of the Paúl da Serra, and you'll enjoy the laughter of a vigorous levada and the falls that feed it.

Start the walk at the left-hand side of the red and white concrete pillars at the ENTRANCE to the **Bica da Cana** refuge. Descend a grassy path through ferns. You skirt to the left of fence posts and the large heath tree grove behind them. In **4min** climb over a stile. Just beyond it, go left at a fork. Continue down beneath a leafy bower. In **12min**, at a T-junction, turn right. (If you look behind you here, you'll

Below Bica da Cana, Pináculo (on the right, in the middle distance) rises above heath trees. Fog engulfs São Vicente's valley, but the peaks in the east (Walk 19) are bathed in sun.

see a blue 'hat' painted on a rock.) Now you're on the fairly overgrown and very wet (even in high summer!) path that will take you to Pináculo.

In **30min** you reach the source of the **Levada da Serra**, where wild carrots and *Senecio* spill down the cliff. In **35min** come to a sign, 'Caramujo' (an old farm) and a few metres beyond it, an *arrow* indicating Caramujo. Our path back up to Bica starts just opposite this arrow, but for now continue on the levada for eight minutes, when you'll come to our favourite lunch spot: here you can sit in long golden grasses ablaze with foxgloves and butterflies, beneath waterfalls foaming down a high and mossy basalt rock face (**43min**). A gentle valley lies before you, leading the eye to São Vicente and the chapel of Nossa Senhora de Fátima (photograph page 19). Hawks circle watchfully above. Just past here is the giant basalt **Pináculo** (**45min**). Continue along the levada as long as you like — perhaps for another 15 minutes — just to enjoy the negative ions, the flowers, and the views.

Before you lose height, turn back. Pass 'the Pinnacle' (**1h 20min**) and, on reaching the *arrow* indicating Caramujo, turn left uphill on a good path (**1h30min**). After passing a stone on your right inscribed 'MN' (**1h40min**), cross a deep gully, then turn left on a path, making for the heights. When you come to a fence, turn right uphill in front of it (there may be a sign here with an orange rectangle and one star). Make for the Bica da Cana viewpoint, where two isolated trees stand out as landmarks (even in fog). Some wind generators are behind you, to your left. The fence turns 90° to the left not far below the viewpoint: continue *straight ahead* uphill through ferns, aiming just to the left of the two isolated trees. You can see a fence ahead; turn right just in front of it. After a few yards a stile (or gap; **1h55min**) gives access to the far side of the fence. Visit the **Bica da Cana** VIEWPOINT (*P*33), then follow the track back to your car at the ENTRANCE (**2h05min**).

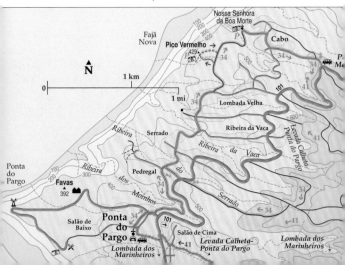

34 CIRCUIT AROUND PONTA DO PARGO

Map opposite; photographs page 135   **Distance:** 10.5km/6.5mi; 4h
Grade: easy, with ascents/descents of 250m/820ft overall. Note that the
levada may be dry outside summer months.
Equipment: stout shoes, sunhat, windproof, fleece, picnic, water
How to get there and return: 🚐 80, 142, 150 or 🚌 (Car tour 6) to/from
Ponta do Pargo, or 🚌 to/from Nossa Senhora da Boa Morte. Even better:
🚐 or 🚌 to the levada crossing north of Lombada dos Marinheiros (see
touring map), do the walk in reverse and return by bus from Ponta do
Pargo (a bit longer, but avoids the tedious climb to the levada).

This lovely ramble follows a country road from Ponta do
Pargo to Cabo and takes in a short stretch of the Levada
Calheta–Ponta do Pargo (see also Walk 41). The only dis-
advantage is the 25-minute climb to the levada; we prefer to
climb on asphalt from Cabo, then descend the unpleasant
rough track to Pedregal. But the best option is to start further
south (see above) and avoid the climb altogether!

Start the walk at the CHURCH in **Ponta do Pargo**. With the
church on your left, walk left down the road signposted to
Salão de Baixo, but turn right immediately, passing the Casa
do Povo. Ignore all paths off left. When you come to a crossroads (to the lighthouse), walk a few paces to the right uphill
but, just before reaching the main ER101, go left downhill,
passing a garage on the left with a tiled door frame. The road
descends, crosses the **Ribeira dos Moinhos**, and rises into
Pedregal, where you pass a tap on the right ('CMC'; **30min**).

Continue along the gently undulating road through
flower-filled **Serrado** (notice the beautifully carved façade of
a house on the right) and then **Lombada Velha**, where a
Canary palm graces the first house and a beautiful old manor
stands off to the left, shaded by a huge eucalyptus. Beyond
this hamlet keep left along an earthen track. It's worth forking
left to the trig point at **Pico Vermelho**, for the view back
towards the lighthouse and Pico das Favas (with the antenna).

The track rises to the chapel of **Nossa Senhora da Boa
Morte** (**1h35min**). This modern building is unremarkable,
but its grassy setting is idyllic — as the contented cows will
agree! There is a *miradouro* nearby. From the chapel follow
the asphalt road uphill through **Cabo** to the ER101. Just *before*
the main road, turn right on the **Levada Calheta–Ponta do
Pargo** (a large water tank is on your left; **2h**). The levada
crosses the main road in seven minutes, then runs inland.
Follow its meanderings for under an hour. Four minutes after
crossing the **Ribeira do Serrado** on a narrow levada 'bridge',
turn right down an eroded jeep track (**3h**). Descend to the
ER101 (by a tap on the right), cross the road and continue
straight down, back to the old road in **Pedregal**. Turn left;
after 40m/yds you pass the tap encountered earlier. Retrace
your steps to **Ponta do Pargo** (**4h**).

35 CAMPO GRANDE • LEVADA DO PAÚL • RABAÇAL • LORETO

Distance: 15km/9.3mi; 4h55min

Grade: moderate, with a slight **possibility of vertigo** on the levada

Equipment: stout shoes (walking boots preferable), sunhat, windproof, fleece, picnic, plastic bottle/water purifying tablets, strong torch

How to get there: 🚌 115 or 142 to Recta das Canhas ('**Ray**-tah dahs **Kahn**-yahs'), where there is a taxi rank. Ask the driver to take you to Cristo Rei, Campo Grande (**Kreesh**-toh Ray, **Kam**-poh Grahnd).
To return: 🚌 80, 115 or 142 from Loreto

Shorter walks

1   Levada do Paúl. Walk as far as you like from Cristo Rei along this levada; perhaps to the caves and back. 5km/3mi; 1h30min. Grade and equipment as above (but no torch needed). Best access is by 🚗 (a detour on Car tour 5). Note that the path may be very wet!

2   Rabaçal — Loreto. 11km/6.8mi; 3h40min. Grade, equipment, access as main walk. Ask the taxi driver to take you to the Rabaçal turn-off on the ER110; join the main walk just after the 1h15min-point.

An awe-inspiring landscape, all stillness and solitude. The flanks of the Paúl da Serra stretch out before you, end-lessly, under a porcelain-blue sky. Only your own shadow and a few sheep will walk with you on the 'marsh of the mountain range'.

The taxi will deposit you on **Campo Grande**, 9km up the road from Canhas, just below a statue of Christ the King ('CRISTO REI'). Here the ER209 crosses the **Levada do Paúl**: there is a small waterhouse on the right and two concrete markers on the left (and perhaps a sign with a green rectangle and one star). This is one of the island's older levadas, now integrated into the new scheme. Further east it is more accurately called the Levada da Bica da Cana, for it takes its source below Bica da Cana, in the Ribeira da Ponta do Sol (Walk 36).

The blue, blue ribbon of the Levada do Paúl

Begin by walking west (*P*35), following the flow of the levada and looking down over the moors to the lush south coast. The levada is ribboning ahead of you — now silver, now amethyst, always mesmerising. There's a narrow bit of path by a waterfall in about five minutes, but no further obstacles. At **25min** pass a river pool, fed by a waterfall; reach a second in **45min**. Here, caves stretch up into the hills on the right (*P*35) — shelter for animals and shepherds in bad weather. In spring the hillside is golden with gorse, the levada mirrors the sky, and a few baby goats dare to gambol along your path. Cows graze freely on the lower slopes.

At **1h10min** you'll see a large building up to the right (the hotel at Urze), as well as a metal pipe in the distance. The pipe is carrying water from the reservoir above Rabaçal down to the Calheta power station. The turbines of this station (commissioned 1953) feed on water from five separate levadas: you are walking one of them now, Walk 38 introduces a second, and Walk 37 explores the other three. From the power station the water is sent eastwards to irrigate the fields of Calheta (14km/8.7mi of channels) and westwards to Ponta do Pargo (40km/25mi of channels). Walks 34 and 41 amble along this levada.

Crossing a road, you come to a tiny chapel beside the levada (**1h15min**). The levada continues into the reservoir, from where it is piped down to the power station. Cross the ER110 (Porto Moniz/ Encumeada road), where you will see the **Levada da Ribeira Grande** (Walk 38) below the road. Walk left, to a large parking area (usually full of souvenir stalls). Here take the narrow road (closed to traffic) down towards Rabaçal. After crossing the **Ribeira do Alecrím** with its lovely pools (**1h25min**), continue downhill under the watchful eyes of goats until you arrive at **Rabaçal**, a government rest house (**1h40min**).

When the tarred road ends, turn right down a dirt track to the **Levada do Risco**. Follow the track beside it for five minutes, then fork left down a path, to the **Levada das 25 Fontes**. Turn left when you reach this levada, following the flow (both of these levadas are explored at leisure in Walk 37). Fifteen minutes' walking along this enchanting watercourse will bring you to a grassy sun-trap outside the entrance to the first major tunnel built on Madeira, in the mid 1800s (notice the poignant shrine). It takes under 20 minutes to pass through this very high tunnel, built to accommodate people on horseback. Unfortunately, today we have to share the path with an intrusive shoulder-high water pipe.

Soon you've left the shade of Rabaçal for the sunny heights of Calheta's *lombos,* where you'll find a keepers' cottage, a rustic picnic table and a tap. *Before* you reach the cottage,

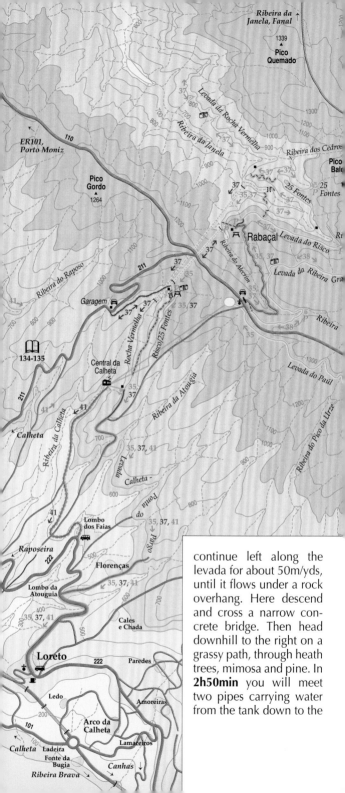

continue left along the levada for about 50m/yds, until it flows under a rock overhang. Here descend and cross a narrow concrete bridge. Then head downhill to the right on a grassy path, through heath trees, mimosa and pine. In **2h50min** you will meet two pipes carrying water from the tank down to the

power station. Five minutes later, a single pipe holds the flow of the levadas of Risco and 25 Fontes. Soon meet the **Levada da Rocha Vermelha** and follow it to a waterhouse and small tank, whence it too shoots down to the power station. *(Alternative walk 37-2 joins here.)*

From here a jeep track takes you to the wide **Levada Calheta–Ponta do Pargo (3h25min)**. Turn left and enjoy a sunny stroll with views over the south coast. Some 35 minutes along, turn right down any road to descend through **Florenças**. Meeting the main ER222 (**4h25min**); turn left and come to **Loreto**'s plane-shaded centre and chapel after **4h55min**. The BUS stops here.

Map begins on pages 124-125; ends on the reverse of the touring map

Distance: 9km/5.6mi; 3h (3h50min if you walk all the way to Cascalho)

Grade: moderate, with a descent and re-ascent of 320m/1050ft; you must be sure-footed and have a head for heights (**possibility of vertigo**).

Equipment: stout shoes (walking boots preferable), fleece, long trousers, sunhat, windproof, picnic, plastic bottle/water purifying tablets, whistle, walking stick, *torch*

How to get there and return: as Picnics 35 and 36, page 16

Alternative walk: Levada da Bica da Cana. 12.5km/7.8mi; 3h. Fairly easy climb/descent of 100m/330ft, but **possibility of vertigo** on the narrow levada path. Equipment, access/return as main walk. Follow the main walk for 40min, then continue on the levada, to climb to its source just below the Paúl da Serra (1h35min). Return the same way.

Cascalho is a primeval wonderland, known only to goats, levada builders and a very few guides and walkers. It's a hidden bowl of waterfalls where the Ribeira da Ponta do Sol gathers its strength. This torrent now feeds the Levada das Rabaças (Walk 32).

Begin the walk on the ER209 below the statue of 'CRISTO REI': head east on the **Levada da Bica da Cana**, walking against the flow (Walk 35 heads west here). The bright blue ribbon of water takes you past a lone pine and collapsed old fireplace on the left (**20min**; *P*36). Three minutes later you cross a beautiful old cobbled trail (this route descends to the ER222 in 9km/6mi; 2h30min). On the far side of the trail the levada path starts to climb. When the climb levels out two minutes later, you enjoy the spectacular view shown below (*P*36) down the **Ribeira da Ponta do Sol**. Below, to the right, you'll spot your track down to Cascalho.

As you continue on the narrow path, you will probably be astounded to see cows and bullocks grazing freely on this extremely precipitous terrain. It is obvious that walkers have not been here in great numbers, so *the safety of this livestock is your responsibility: go slowly and very quietly!*

At **40min** you come to the stony crossing track seen from above: turn down right. The descent is quite gradual, but the rubble underfoot is treacherous. Water, which has been pouring down beside the track in gullies, is soon channelled into a levada. At under **1h** you come to a promontory and a WORKMEN'S SHED. From here there is a superb view down over Lombada on a hilltop in the valley, with its rosy *solar* and white chapel (Walk 30). Continue through the short S-shaped TUNNEL at the left of the shed, and *use your torch:* the levada *crosses* the track in the tunnel.

Picnic 36 can overlook the Ribeira da Ponta do Sol

*The Alternative walk climbs 100m/330ft to the source of the levada, sometimes on steps. Experienced walkers, **equipped with a compass**, could scramble from the source up the river bed and make their way to Bica da Cana, to be met by friends (see map on reverse of touring map). But for the average walker, who has left a car at Cristo Rei, this would be **exceedingly dangerous**: fog comes down like a curtain! Remember, the levada is your **only** guide back to your car, and it is unlikely that you would be able to find it again.*

Out of the tunnel, you soon reach a huge basin; the well-channelled levada drops here. You could be forgiven for thinking yourself already at Cascalho … but it is still hidden. Continue downhill with the levada, past a sluice, tunnel and water pit (**1h15min**). Some cable fencing allays feelings of vertigo now. This is a most exhilarating part of the walk, beside the rushing water. Finally, at **1h20min**, you round another bend and look ahead to **Cascalho**, the *caldeirão* at the head of the Ribeira da Ponta do Sol (allow an additional 20 minutes, if you walk on to the waterfalls and tunnel). Chances are that you'll be enveloped in mist by midday, but in summer the bowl is a suntrap — an exquisite picnic spot.

Return the same way to the ER209 (**3h-3h50min**).

37 RABAÇAL'S LEVADAS

Map pages 124-125   **Distance:** 16km/10mi; 5h

Grade: fairly strenuous, with descents/re-ascents of 400m/1300ft; you must be sure-footed and have a head for heights (**possibility of vertigo**)

Equipment: stout shoes (walking boots preferable), fleece, long trousers, sunhat, windproof, whistle, rainhat, picnic, plastic bottle/water purifying tablets

How to get there and return: 🚗 car (Car tour 5) or taxi (from the Recta das Canhas; see Walk 35, page 122) to the parking area on the ER110, at the top of the road to Rabaçal (the road itself is closed to traffic). *Note: While this is the usual approach to Rabaçal, the 200m/650ft climb from the houses back to the ER110 (2km; 45min) can be very tiring; we prefer to park as for Alternative walk 1 below.*

Shorter walks (both involve a 200m/650ft climb back from Rabaçal)

1 Rabaçal — Risco — Rabaçal. 5.7km/3.5mi; 1h45min. Moderate. Access as above. Follow the main walk to Risco; return the same way.

2 Rabaçal — 25 Fontes — Rabaçal. 9km/5.6mi; 2h55min. Moderate; the vertiginous stretches are protected by wooden fencing. Access as above. Follow the main walk for 35min, then turn left down the path to the Levada das 25 Fontes. Do the main walk from the 51min-point to 25 Fontes and return the same way.

Alternative walks

1 Rabaçal tunnel — Rabaçal levadas — Rabaçal tunnel. 16km/10mi; 5h15min. Grade and equipment as main walk; take a *torch* as well. Access by 🚗. You may prefer this approach, to avoid the tiring climb back up from Rabaçal. From the ER110 drive south on the ER211 and park about 2km downhill, by a derelict garage (now just a wall; 'Garagem' on the map). From there follow the dirt track on the opposite side of the road to the Rabaçal tunnel (*P*37c; 10min) and go through it (20min). You emerge at a sun-trap on the Levada das 25 Fontes (*P*37b). Follow the levada for a minute, then turn right up steps to the Risco levada and Rabaçal. Do the main walk, but don't climb back up to Rabaçal; return to the sun-trap and go through the tunnel, back to your car.

2 Rabaçal levadas — Rocha Vermelha tunnel — Loreto. 22.5km/14mi; about 6h30min. Grade: moderate, but you must be sure-footed and have a head for heights (**danger of vertigo** just before the tunnel). Equipment as main walk, plus torch. Access by taxi (see Walk 35, page 122); return on 🚌 80, 115 or 142 from Loreto. Follow the main walk to the 3h35min-point; then, instead of climbing up to Rabaçal, continue through the Rocha Vermelha tunnel (20min), coming out in the Calheta Valley. Follow the levada to its tiny reservoir, then pick up Walk 35 to continue to Loreto (see page 124, just after the 2h50min-point).

Rabaçal is an enchanted fairyland of singing waterfalls, a favourite excursion spot for the islanders. Here at the head of Madeira's greatest valley, the Rabaçal house (*P*37a) lies dwarfed beneath emerald mountains. Three levadas converge here; each has its own 'personality', and this walk lets you make friends with all three.

   The walk begins at the PARKING AREA on the ER110 above Rabaçal. Walk down to the **Rabaçal** houses (**30min**) and turn right down a dirt track, to join the highest levada (1030m/3380ft), the **Levada do Risco**. Pass a fork to the Levada das

Mossy trail beside the Levada do Risco. Notice how some of the heath trees grow out horizontally across the levada.

25 Fontes in **35min** and in **39min** ford a spillway created by a waterfall on the right. Around here the levada is flanked by an exceedingly beautiful mossy 'carpet' (see above), and the banks are built up high to cope with a great flow. At a fork, keep right on concrete to a viewpoint in a typical *caldeirão* (**43min**; *P*37d), where the **Risco** waterfall cascades into a pool from a height of 100m/325ft. A tunnel on the right disgorges even more water, drawn from below the Urze peak. From here you can see the levada continue around the head of the gorge and along the valley opposite to its source, but this dangerous route is closed to walkers. Look below, across the valley, to see a second channel cut into the mountainside: this is the 'middle' levada, leading to 25 Fontes ('25 Springs').

Now retrace your steps to the fork to 25 Fontes (**51min**). Turn right and descend stone steps to reach the **Levada das 25 Fontes** (altitude 960m/3150ft). Turn right and you will see the Risco waterfall again, from a lower level: in **1h10min** you come to the head of the gorge where it dives down. Then cross the bed of the **Ribeira Grande**, to meet a tiny waterhouse: water is usually gushing out of its front door… From here on the levada channel is only 30cm/1ft wide in places, and there are drops at the left of up to 30m/100ft. But even without fencing we never found this levada vertiginous because, unlike most others, it is built up off the path, not sunk into it. The concrete edge of the levada is at waist level, and you can hold on to it for moral support if the drops worry you. It's cooling to run your hands in the water on a hot day.

In **1h30min** you pass the path down left to the Levada da Rocha Vermelha; ignore it for now. In about **1h40min**, in a tributary of the Cedros River, you reach a path leading up right (by a sluice), and at once you see the '**Vinte e Cinco' (25) Fontes** — a semi-circular bowl into which tumble down many sparkling waterfalls (but, alas, no longer 25). It's a lovely place to paddle under ferns (**P**37e).

From here return to the path passed 10 minutes earlier. Turn down right (perhaps passing some beehives on your right). Keep to the main zigzag path to prevent erosion. The **Levada da Rocha Vermelha** (**2h05min**), at 850m/2790ft, is the lowest of the Rabaçal levadas. A keepers' house sits below on your right. This levada is much wider than the other two and is the newest of the three. Turn right on it, back up into the valley of the **Ribeira dos Cedros**. There are waterfalls left, right and centre! You cross the Cedros ravine on the levada channel (covered with concrete slabs), and find a tunnel on your right: water is flowing in from mountains on the east side of the Seixal River, some 4km/2.5mi away. Turn left on the levada and follow it round the valley. Soon you're just opposite the *levadeiros'* house; some 200m/650ft directly above it you see the Rabaçal houses. Notice how the levada narrows beyond each tributary, as you head towards its source. In **2h40min** you might like to take a break at a grassy promontory, from where there is a magnificent view of the Ribeira da Janela 200m/650ft below.

Time constraints will limit the distance you can walk on this levada; we stop after **2h55min**, where the thick blue line ends on the map*. From here return the same way, enjoying grassy verges and the aroma of wild mint, open views and shady heath-tree bowers. You'll be back at the keepers' cottage in **3h25min**. Stay on the levada, passing the path where you came down to it, and turning up into the **Ribeira Grande**. The Risco falls and the 25 Fontes Levada are visible ahead and above you. Across this wild gully yawns the Rocha Vermelha tunnel (Alternative walk 2); it disgorges in the Calheta Valley near the path of Walk 35.

A bridge crosses the river, to the tunnel, but carry on past it, to the sluices and rock pools (**3h35min**), where you can take a break below the roaring (Risco) falls. Then walk back, cross the bridge, and turn *sharp left* up a stone-laid path (masked by ferns at first), to begin the climb back to Rabaçal. In 15 minutes you reach the **Levada das 25 Fontes**, where you turn right. Ten minutes later, just before a high tunnel (Walk 35), steps on the left take you up to the picnic area at **Rabaçal** (**4h15min**). From here it's a tiring slog of about 45 minutes back up to the CAR PARK (**5h**).

*About 15 minutes further on, you would find steps similar to those in the photograph on page 127 — but almost 300 of them! **Experts** might like to climb them (the descent is horrendously vertiginous) and pursue the levada to its source (another 50min; *not* shown on the map).

38 LEVADA DA RIBEIRA GRANDE

See map on pages 124-125   **Distance:** 6km/3.7mi; 1h50min

Grade: easy, but some of the clay paths are very slippery; you must be sure-footed and have a head for heights (slight **possibility of vertigo**).

Equipment: stout shoes, picnic, water

How to get there and return: 🚗 car to the parking area on the ER110, at the top of the road to Rabaçal (Car tour 5)

Here's a short ramble that is easily combined with a day's touring on the Paúl da Serra. Since this levada is not named on any maps, we have tried to christen it appropriately: it takes its source in the Ribeira Grande, almost 300m/1000ft above the levadas followed in Walk 37. At 1300m/4265ft, this is the 'penthouse suite' of the Ribeira Grande levadas. But unlike the levadas in Walk 37, this one is twinned with the Levada do Paúl (Walk 35) and flows into the reservoir on the ER110.

Start out at the car park: walk down the Rabaçal road for 120m/yds, then fork right on a path. This takes you to the wide **Levada da Ribeira Grande**. A pretty amble brings you quickly to a small semi-circular reservoir, which may be brimming with tiny trout (**12min**; *P*38). Immediately past it, you cross the **Ribeira do Alecrím** (Rosemary River).

After a narrow, unprotected stretch with a sheer drop to the left (amply wide and quickly passed), you come to 50 shallow STEPS beside a water chute (like the one in the photograph at the top of page 127). These steps take you up to a fine viewpoint over the Ribeira da Janela and your starting point (**30min**) and then into the valley of the **Ribeira Grande**, from where you will have glimpses down to the three levadas followed in Walk 37.

When you reach the source of the levada in the wide river bed (**55min**), a waterfall, rock pools and bird song beckon you to bide a while. Then return the same way to the CAR PARK on the ER110 (**1h50min**).

Rock pools and waterfall in the bed of the Ribeira Grande

See map pages 124-125

Distance: 4km/2.5mi; 1h15min

Grade: easy climb/descent of 150m/ 500ft, but avoid the climb to the summit if there is any sign of mist descending; follow the levada to find your way back to your car.

Equipment: stout shoes, sunhat, picnic, water

How to get there and return: 🚗 car to the junction of the ER110 to Bica da Cana and the ER208 to Estanquinhos, by a narrow levada (Car tour 5)

Photograph: Pico Ruivo do Paúl, from the Estanquinhos/ Bica da Cana junction

By now it won't be a secret to you that the Paúl da Serra is one of our favourite places on Madeira — and with the new expressway you're there in a trice. Wonderful for picnicking and doing a few short walks on a 'lazy day'. This is another stunner!

Start out at the road JUNCTION: head north in the setting shown above, following the grassy banks beside the narrow blue ribbon of levada. The levada squiggles its way through woods (**10min**) and eventually crosses a track at a beautiful picnic setting (*P*39). Just three minutes later, beyond the water collection pit shown below, you reach the source of the levada (**20min**). From here just follow the trampled bracken up to the top of **Pico Ruivo do Paúl** (**30min** — or even **45min** on a hot day). From here there is a wonderful view east, similar to the view in the photograph on page 119.

Rather than return the same way, head south down the hill and make your way (no particular path) over the moorland, back to your car at the JUNCTION (**1h15min**).

View towards the Janela Valley from the water pit

40 FROM PRAZERES TO PAÚL DO MAR

Map pages 134-135, photo page 15   Distance: 5km/3mi; 1h35min

Grade: strenuous descent of about 550m/1800ft *in full sun*; you must be sure-footed and have a head for heights (**danger of vertigo**). *Avoid in damp weather, when the path would be slippery and treacherous.*
Note: To do the walk in reverse (easier on the knees and less vertiginous), walk through a narrow gap between houses, a few metres/yards uphill from the bar on the quay in Paúl do Mar, *before* the road bends left.
Equipment: stout shoes (walking boots preferable), sunhat, whistle, walking stick, picnic, water; extra fleece and windproof in cool weather
How to get there: 🚌 142 or 🚗 to Prazeres; by car, park at the Hotel Jardim Atlántico (a detour on Car tour 6)
To return: 🚕 taxi from Paúl do Mar back to your car, or to the ER101 in time for the return 🚌 142. Book a taxi at the office/bar by the church in Prazeres (there *are* taxis at Paúl do Mar, but they are sometimes away on day trips). Alternatively, climb back up to Prazeres (exhausting on a hot day), *if you are sure you can catch your return bus!*
Note: There are several other cliff-side routes on the southwest coast, but some are hard to locate and not well maintained. They are only recommended for very experienced walkers with a head for heights. These hikes are best suited to those staying at the Hotel Jardim Atlántico, where you can get a route map and advice on the viability of the paths.

This is *the* five-star route on the southwest coast, a wonderfully exhilarating descent that spirals you down to photogenic Paúl do Mar. The focal points are the ochre-to-burgundy volcanic cliffs, a Swiss cheese landscape of caves and rivulets plastered with houseleeks and Pride of Madeira. Take plenty of film!

Begin on the ER222 at **Prazeres**. Follow the signposted road through bucolic countryside to the HOTEL JARDIM ATLÁNTICO (**30min**). At the far end of the hotel car park, walk south downhill on a concrete pavement with lamp-posts (signposted 'VEREDA DO PAÚL'). Already there are wonderful views over Jardim do Mar to the left and Paúl do Mar below. Soon steps take you down to an exquisite old cobbled trail. Some 10 minutes down, someone has thoughtfully placed a bench below pines, where you can sit and contemplate the fields and terraces below Maloeira on the plateau and Raposeira on the ridge beyond it (*P*40).

Soon the path goes into a roller-coaster descent and, just when you think you cannot stomach the pitch any longer, you're saved from the abyss by a zig or a zag. As you near the sea, look back into the great cleft where the Seca and Cova rivers come together and plummet 400m/1300ft in a graceful waterfall. After crossing a stone bridge over the **Ribeira Seca** in a delightful setting, descend for another five minutes, then turn down left to the tiny quay at **Paúl do Mar** (**1h35min**), where the falls crash onto the pebbly shore just behind the colourful fishing boats.

If you haven't arranged for someone to collect you, walk on to the restaurant, where they can call a taxi.

41 LEVADA CALHETA–PONTA DO PARGO

See also maps on pages 120 and 124-125, and the touring map

Grade: easy   **Distance:** as individual walk suggestions

Equipment: stout shoes, sunhat, picnic, water

How to get there: 🚌 142 or 🚗 to Raposeira
To return: 🚌 back to your base or your car; see opposite

The Levada Calheta–Ponta do Pargo (see notes on page 123) is just perfect for strolling. As it contours along the sun-drenched plains above the coast, it gives you superb views up to the Paúl da Serra, where scudding clouds create an ever-changing mosaic on the hillsides. Gorgeous all year round, these walks are at their best in high summer, when the levada is full to brimming, and the agapanthus and hydrangeas are in bloom (in winter, the levada is sometimes empty). You stroll under pine and eucalyptus, by ferny glens and banks of lilies. While there is ample shade, much of the route is exposed; adequate sun protection is *essential*.

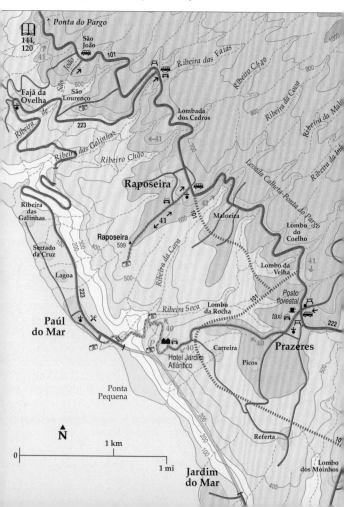

Walks 34 and 41: the Levada Calheta–Ponta do Pargo in July; you'll be a source of some curiosity to the locals!

Walk suggestions: Both of our suggestions begin below (just south of) Raposeira church, but you can join the **Levada Calheta–Ponta do Pargo** at other convenient points. The touring map shows you at a glance where the levada crosses the road. If you are driving, there are several places to park along the quiet ER101, for example 2km west of Raposeira church, at the turn-off down to Fajã da Ovelha. Perhaps combine your levada walk with a visit to the fine viewpoint over Paúl do Mar at Raposeira (2km return), or just amble down one of the grassy trails overlooking the lighthouse at Ponta do Pargo.

1   Follow the levada east from Raposeira. You can leave it for the ER222 at Prazeres (4.7km/3mi; 1h15min), Lombo dos Moinhos (9km/ 5.6mi; 2h15min), or the power station above Calheta (20.5km/12.7mi; 5h). Beyond the power station you could join Walk 35 and continue to Loreto (26.5km/16.5mi; 6h30min; map pages 124-125, notes page 125). This eastern stretch is only served by 🚐 142 at time of writing.

2   Head west from Raposeira (see below and touring map; see also Walk 34 on page 121). You cross the road at Lombada dos Marinheiros (9km/5.6mi; 2h15min; 🚐 80, 142), but must descend to Ponta do Pargo (15km/ 9.3mi; 3h45min; 🚐 80, 142, 150). The levada ends above Cabo, on the route of Walk 34 (21.5km/13.3mi; 5h20min; 🚐 80, 142, 150).

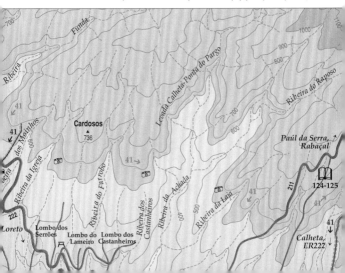

42 LEVADA DA CENTRAL DA RIBEIRA DA JANELA

Distance: up to 9km/5.6mi; 2h30min

Grade: easy, but you must be sure-footed and have a head for heights; **possibility of vertigo.**

Equipment: stout shoes (walking boots preferable), long trousers, fleece, windproof, sunhat, rainhat, picnic, water, whistle, *optional torch*

How to get there and return: 🚗 car or taxi to the reservoir above Porto Moniz. Ask a taxi driver for 'Levada da Central'. By car, drive towards Santa on the EN101 and turn off left for 'Lamaceiros' 3.5km up from the roundabout by the petrol station. Keep straight on past any forks. After 1km you pass to the left of the church/bus stop at Lamaceiros. When the road bends right after a further 300m, go straight ahead and park at the recreation area by the levada. Or 🚌 80, 139 or 150 to the church at Lamaceiros and walk on to the levada; same buses to return.

Short walk: to the second filtration point and back. 3.5km/2.2mi; 1h. Easy. Follow the main walk for 30min and return the same way.

From the western flanks of the great Janela Valley you look across to the stupendous array of tiny terraces tumbling helter-skelter from Ribeira da Janela down to the river far below. Then you leave the cultivation behind, for ferny glens, mossy cliffs and primeval woodlands.

Start out at the RESERVOIR IN THE RECREATION AREA and follow the wide **Levada da Central da Ribeira da Janela** (inaugur-

In about 30 minutes the levada widens by a second filtration point. The path is lined with fruit trees intertwined with passion flowers. This is an especially beautiful picnic spot (a second setting for Picnic 42). Further along you'll walk beneath beech trees and indigenous laurels and skirt high escarpments bearded with a great variety of ferns.

ated 1965) past a picnic table (**3min**; **P**42) and a then a wide filtration point. Huge bushes of fennel, apple and fig trees, and garlands of passion flowers herald the next filtration tank (**30min**; **P**42). Five minutes later, notice the cables and pulleys used for moving supplies between the watercourse and the valley floor. Down by the river one of the most impressive expanses of terracing on the island stretches out below you.

Within **45min** the sure of foot will reach a ferny glen in the upper reaches of the **Ribeira da Cova Negra**. Soon you skirt a rock wall pouring with rainwater. In **1h** you are looking straight up the Janela Valley; if you have binoculars, you will easily see the Rabaçal houses from here (Walks 35 and 37).

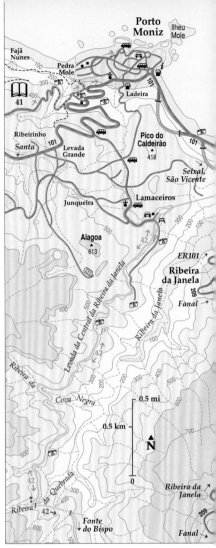

The walk ends in **1h15min**, when you meet a tunnel* in the **Ribeira da Quebrada**. Turn back here, to catch the bus or return to your car near the RESERVOIR (**2h30min**).

*It takes 10 minutes to get through this tunnel, but there are seven more behind it, one of which takes about 30 minutes. *Experts* could follow the *extremely vertiginous* levada to the keepers' house and then the source (about 2h30min from here; strong torch and raingear needed … but you will get soaked anyway). From the keepers' house a steep path, then a track climbs 850m/2800ft (7km/4.3mi; about 3h) to Fonte do Bispo. This route is *not* shown on any of our maps. Arrange to be met on the ER110 at the 'Galhano' signpost, opposite Fonte do Bispo (Car tour 5).

BUS TIMETABLES

Below is a list of destinations serving the walks in this book. Numbers following place names are *bus numbers;* they are arranged below in numerical order. *But note that all orange 'town' buses are on page 142.* See page 9 for more bus information and pages 10-11 for bus departure points. Note that where intermediate times are shown, they are **approximate: arrive early! No buses run on Christmas day.**

Achadinha 111
Águas Mansas 60, 77, 110
Arco de São Jorge 6, 103, 132
Assomada 2, 20, 23, 25, 53, 56, 78, 103, 113, 138
Babosas *town* 🚌 22
Barreira *shuttle* 🚌 91
Boa Morte 127, 148
Boaventura 6, 132
Boqueirão 60, 110
Cabo Girão 154
Camacha 29, 77
Campanário 6, 7, 115, 123, 139, 142, 148
Canhas 115, 142
Caniçal 113
Corticeiras 96
Cruz 53, 78
Cruzinhas 56, 103, 138
Curral das Freiras 81
Eira do Serrado (turn-off) 81
Encumeada 6, 139
Estreito de C.d. Lobos 3, 6, 7, 96§, 115, 123, 139, 142, 148, 154

Faial 53, 56, 78, 103, 138
Fonte Vermelha, Bar 156
Fontes 127, 148
Formiga 115, 142
Ilha de São Jorge 103, 132, 138
Jardim Botânico *town* 🚌 29, 30, 31
Lamaceiros 80, 139, 150
Lombo Grande 60
Loreto 115, 142
Machico 20, 23, 53, 56, 78, 113, 156
Madeira Shopping *town* 🚌 8, 8a, 16, 150
Monte 56, 103, 138, *town* 🚌 20, 21
Nogueira 110, 114
Palheiro Ferreiro 29, 77, *town* 🚌 36, 37, 47
Paúl do Mar 80, 115
Pico do Facho (turn-off to) 113
Poiso 56, 103, 138
Ponta do Pargo 80, 139, 142
Ponta do Sol 80 (direct); or

115, 142 (via the ER222)
Portela 53, 78
Porto da Cruz 53, 56, 78, 103, 138, 156
Porto Moniz 80, 139, 150
Prazeres 142
Raposeira 142
Ribeira Brava 6, 7, 80, 115, 127, 139, 142
Ribeira Seca 113
Ribeirinha 111
Ribeiro Frio 56, 103, 138
Romeiros *town* 🚌 29
Santa 80, 139, 142, 150
Santana 56, 103, 132, 138
Santo da Serra 20, 77, 78
São João Latrão *town* 🚌 47
São Jorge 103, 132, 138
São Lourenço Point 113
São Vicente 6, 80, 139, 150
Sítio Quatro Estradas 77
Stadium *town* 🚌 45
Trapiche *town* 🚌 10A, 11; *shuttle* 🚌 91
Vale Paraíso 29, 77

2 Funchal • Assomada (journey time 35min)
Departs Funchal: 07.30, 08.20+, 08.30§, 09.15+, 10.00, 11.00, 11.35+, 11.45□, 12.00•, 12.10+, 14.00*, 15.00, 16.00*, 16.30•, 17.00*, 17.45*, 18.00•, 18.45*, 19.00•, 19.30*, 20.15*, 20.30•, 21.00*, 22.30, 23.45

Departs Assomada: 06.45•, 07.00*, 07.30*, 08.10*, 08.30•, 09.10+, 09.30§, 09.55+, 11.00, 11.40*, 12.00•, 12.15+, 12.25□, 13.00•, 13.30•, 13.45*, 14.40*, 14.45+, 15.40, 16.40*, 17.00•, 17.45, 18.30*, 19.00•, 19.30*, 21.10+, 21.30§, 21.45+, 23.10

3 Funchal • Estreito de Câmara de Lobos (journey time 45min)
Departs Funchal: 07.45□, 08.45•, 08.55□, 10.30+, 11.45§, 11.55+, 12.45, 14.05+, 14.45§, 15.00+, 15.45§, 16.10+, 16.45□, 17.00•, 17.30□, 18.00□, 18.15+, 18.45□, 19.15+, 19.45§, 00.45§

Departs Estreito (a): 06.50+, 07.05□, 07.20+, 07.35+, 08.05+, 08.30*, 08.50§, 09.55§, 10.05+, 11.35+, 12.55§, 13.05§, 13.40§, 14.00+, 15.10•, 15.40□, 15.55•, 16.20+, 16.55§, 17.05+, 17.40□, 18.05•, 20.40§, 22.45

6 Funchal • Arco de São Jorge (via Estreito, Campanário, Ribeira Brava, São Vicente)

Funchal	07.35				13.35*		15.30•	17.35(b)
Ribeira Brava	08.50				14.50*		16.45•	18.50
Encumeada	09.30				15.30*		00.00 ≶	19.30
São Vicente	09.50	11.00+	13.15+	15.30+¶	15.50*	17.00+¶	17.15•	19.50
P. Delgada	10.05	11.15+	13.30+	15.50+¶	16.05*	17.15+¶	17.30•	20.05
Boaventura	10.45	11.25+	13.40+	16.00+¶	16.45*	17.20+¶	17.35•	21.00
Arco S. Jorge	11.30	11.45+					17.50+¶	21.20
							17.50+¶	
Arco S. Jorge		06.40	11.50+		14.30	17.50+¶	17.50•	18.30+¶
Boaventura	05.50+	06.55	12.15+	14.30+	14.45	18.05+¶	18.05•	18.40+¶
P. Delgada	06.20+	07.25	12.45+	14.40+	15.15	18.15+¶	18.15•	18.50+¶
S. Vicente	06.35+	08.00	13.00+	14.55+	15.30	18.25+¶	18.25•	19.10+¶
Encumeada	00.00 ≶	00.00 ≶			16.00		00.00 ≶	
Ribeira Brava	07.30+	08.40			16.30(b)		19.00•	
Funchal	08.30+	09.20			17.40		20.10•	

(a) Departures do not *start* from Estreito; departure times have been estimated and may be as much as 15min *later;* (b) Via the Via Rápida; does not call at Estreito or Campanário; *see other symbol codes opposite.*

7 Funchal · Ribeira Brava (journey time 1h30min)

Departs Funchal: 06.45•, 07.55+⌇, 09.00+⌇, 09.30+, 10.05•, 10.50•, 11.00*, 11.00 ⌇, 12.05•, 13.30□•, 14.00+⌇, 15.30, 17.00, 18.00+⌇, 18.15+⌇, 18.30▪, 20.15, 21.15•, 22.15, 23.30

Departs Ribeira Brava: 06.05, 07.00+⌇, 07.15+⌇, 07.30+⌇, 08.05*, 08.15+⌇, 08.45+⌇, 09.00+⌇, 09.05□ ⌇, 10.10+⌇, 11.00*, 11.45•, 12.00+⌇, 12.35+, 13.35•, 14.30+⌇, 15.30+⌇, 17.30*, 18.35, 19.00 ⌇, 22.10

20 Funchal · Machico · Santo da Serra (via Gaula and Machico)

Funchal	07.15*	09.30+	12.40	16.30+	19.15+	20.45+
Machico	08.00*	10.20+	13.25	17.25+	19.55+	21.30+
Santo da Serra *(arrives)*	08.35*	10.55+	14.05	18.25+	20.30+	22.00+
Santo da Serra *(departs)*	06.30	08.00*	09.45	12.30+	14.45+	16.15•
Machico	07.00	08.45*	10.25	13.05+	15.20+	17.00•
Funchal	07.45	09.30*	11.15	13.55+	16.15+	17.45•

23 Funchal · Machico (journey time 35min direct express, 55min via Gaula)

Departs Funchal: 11.30+ until 15.30+ hourly on the hour, then half-hourly until 19.00+ *(all express);* then 21.30* (via Gaula)

Departs Machico: 06.30+ until 09.00 half-hourly, then 10.00+, 11.30+, 12.30+, 13.30+, and 14.00+ until 17.00 half-hourly *(all express);* also 07.30*, 09.30□, 14.25□, 22.45* *(all via Gaula)*

29 Funchal · Camacha (journey time 45min)

Departs Funchal: 08.00+, 08.15□, 09.00, 10.00, 11.00, 11.40*, 12.15+, 12.30•, 13.00+, 13.25□, 13.30#, 14.30, 15.30, 17.00, 17.30*, 18.00#, 18.15+, 18.30*, 18.40+¶, 18.50+, 19.00, 19.30+, 19.50*, 20.00#, 20.25□, 20.30•, 22.00, 22.30

Departs Camacha: 06.45□, 07.00#, 07.05+, 07.15+, 07.30+, 08.05□, 08.15#, 08.45*, 09.45, 10.45, 11.45, 12.25*, 13.00+, 13.15§, 13.45+, 14.15, 15.15, 16.15, 17.40, 18.15*, 18.45#, 19.15*, 19.45, 21.00§, 22.45

53 Funchal · ⚓ · Machico · Ribeira de Machico · Portela · Porto da Cruz · Faial

Funchal		10.00*	13.15*			17.20*	18.15•	18.20+
Machico	09.00•	10.50*	14.05•	14.30+	15.30+	18.00*	19.00•	19.00+
Portela	09.25•	11.15•	14.20•	14.50+	15.50+	18.25*	19.25•	19.25+
Pto Cruz	09.35•	11.30•	14.35•	15.05•	16.20+	19.35*	19.35•	19.35+
Faial *(arr)*	09.45•	11.45•	14.45•	15.15•		18.45•	19.45•	19.45+
Faial *(dep)*	05.45+	07.40+	10.15	13.00	13.30•	15.30*	17.15*	18.20+
Pto Cruz	05.55+	08.05+	10.25	13.10	13.40•	15.40*	17.25*	18.35+
Portela	06.10+	08.20+	10.40	13.25	13.55•	15.55*	17.40*	18.50+
Machico	06.30+	08.40+	11.00	13.50	14.30•	16.30*	18.00*	19.15+
Funchal	07.05+	09.30+	12.00	14.45	15.20•	17.20*	18.45*	20.05+

56 Funchal · Faial · Santana (routing varies; see a-d)

Funchal	08.10+a	09.30□a	10.00+c	10.30•c	12.20+b	14.00□b/d	17.05+b/d
Faial	09.20+a	10.45□a	11.15+c	11.45•c	13.45+b	15.30□b/d	18.35+b/d
Santana	10.00+a	11.00□a	11.30+c	12.00•c	14.00+b		00.00
Santana		11.00+a	12.00□b	13.00+b	15.30#b		
Faial	06.30*b/d	11.10+a	12.15□b	13.30+b	15.45#b		
Funchal	07.50*b/d	13.00+a	13.40□b	14.50+b	17.10#b		

a: northbound via Poiso, Ribeiro Frio, São Roque; southbound via São Roque, Ribeiro Frio, Poiso
b: northbound via Porto da Cruz, São Roque, Cruzinhas; southbound via Cruzinhas, São Roque, Porto da Cruz
c: via Poiso, Ribeiro Frio, Cruzinhas
d: terminates/begins at Faial

60 Funchal · Boqueirão (via Gaula; journey time 1h)

Departs Funchal: 11.00, 13.30*, 17.00+, 18.25+, 19.15, 20.30+
Buses pass Gaula approx. 10min and Lombo Grande 5min before Boqueirão.

Departs Boqueirão: 06.15*, 06.30+, 06.45+, 07.30*, 08.30*, 12.00*, 17.00§
Buses pass Lombo Grande approx. 5min and Gaula 10min after Boqueirão.

00.00 no service; +Mon-Fri; ▪not on 31 Dec or 1 Jan; □only Saturdays; *not Sundays or holidays; ‡only Mon/Wed/Fri; •only Sundays/holidays; ••only Sundays; †not Sundays or the first Saturday in Sept.; #not Saturdays; §Sat/Sun/holidays only; ¶in the school season only; ✢except 1, 6 Jan, 25, 26 Dec, via the coastal road and Ponta do Sol; **only on holidays; ▲Mondays to Saturdays, also holidays; ++Tue, Wed, Thur, Fri only; ⌇ via the Via Rápida and/or the Encumeada Tunnel

77 Funchal · Santo da Serra (via Camacha)

Funchal	07.35*	08.30•	10.30	14.00	16.30	18.00*	19.15#
Camacha	08.10*	09.10•	11.10	14.40	17.10	18.40*	19.55#
Sítio Quatro Estradas	08.40*	09.40•	11.40	15.10	17.40	19.10*	20.25#
Santo da Serra (arrives)	08.50*	09.50•	11.50	15.20	17.50	19.20*	20.35#
Santo da Serra (departs)	07.00	09.00*	10.00•	12.00#	16.15	18.00	20.30+
Sítio Quatro Estradas	07.05	09.05*	10.05•	12.05#	16.20	18.05	20.35+
Camacha	07.40	09.40*	10.40•	12.40#	16.55	18.40	21.10+
Funchal	08.20	10.20*	11.20•	13.20#	17.35	19.20	21.50+

78 Funchal · Machico · Faial (via Santo da Serra and Portela); routing varies; see a-d

Funchal	08.00•a	12.40**b		16.30□d	Faial	06.45▲	17.30•
Machico	08.50•a	13.25**b	17.00+c	17.15□d	Machico	07.45▲	18.30•
Faial (arr)			18.00+c	18.30□d	Funchal (arr)	08.35▲	19.30•

a: via Gaula; terminates at Porto da Cruz (09.40); b: via the airport; terminates at Porto da Cruz (14.15); c: from Machico; terminates at Porto da Cruz; d: via Gaula and the airport

80 Funchal · Porto Moniz (via Ponta do Pargo, Paúl do Mar, Santa and Lamaceiros; see also bus 139 for a 'round the island' trip

Funchal (departs) 10.00+↗; Ribeira Brava 10.50; Calheta 11.30; Paul do Mar 12.00; Ponta do Pargo 12.20; Santa 12.50; Porto Moniz 13.00

Porto Moniz (departs) 16.00+; Ponta do Pargo 16.50; Calheta (10min stop); Ponta do Sol; Ribeira Brava (10min stop); Câmara de Lobos; Funchal (20.00).

81 Funchal · Curral das Freiras (via Eira do Serrado turn-off; journey time 45min)

Departs Funchal: 06.40•, 07.35*, 08.45*, 09.05•, 10.30*, 11.30*, 11.40•, 13.15, 15.05+, 16.30, 17.30+, 18.30+, 19.30, 20.30+, 21.45, 23.45

Departs Curral (from Lombo Chão terminus): 06.20+, 06.30*, 06.40+, 07.30+, 07.40+, 08.45*, 10.00*, 10.30+, 11.45+, 12.00□, 12.50•, 13.15*, 14.30, 16.15+, 17.45, 19.35+, 20.30, 21.30+

96 Funchal · Jardim da Serra (via Estreito de Câmara de Lobos; journey time 1h)

Departs Funchal: 07.00•, 07.30+, 08.05, 09.05, 09.45+ 11.15*, 12.15+*, 13.05*, 14.15+, 15.05, 16.05, 17.30, 18.30+, 18.45, 19.15+, 19.50§, 20.15+, 21.15

Departs Jardim da Serra: 06.30, 06.45*, 07.00+, 08.00, 08.45+, 09.00, 10.15, 11.00+, 12.30□, 12.45+, 13.30+, 14.00□, 14.30+, 15.30+, 16.05§, 16.30+, 17.05§, 17.30+, 18.00+, 18.35§, 20.00

103 Funchal · Santana · Arco de São Jorge (routing varies; see a-d below)

Funchal	07.30+a	07.30§b	13.30+b	13.30□a	16.00*a/c	18.00+a	18.00§a
Pto da Cruz	08.15+a	00.00	00.00	14.15□a	16.40*a/c	18.45+a	00.00
Ribeiro Frio	00.00	08.15§b	14.15+b	00.00	00.00	00.00	18.50§b
Santana	09.40+a	09.15§b	15.00+b	14.45□a	17.10*a/c	19.20+a	19.40§b
Arco	10.55+a	10.25§b	15.55+b	15.35□a	18.00*a/c	19.35+a	20.40§b
Arco	06.00+b	06.20+a	07.20*a	07.20•b	12.30*a	16.30b/d	
Santana	06.45□b	07.05+a	08.30*a	08.25•b	13.25*a	17.30b/d	
Ribeiro Frio	07.30□b	00.00	00.00	09.10□b	00.00	18.35b/d	
Pto da Cruz	00.00	07.30+a	09.05*a	00.00	13.50*a	00.00	
Funchal	08.30□b	08.15+a	09.55*a	10.05•b	14.40*a	19.35b/d	

a: northbound via Porto da Cruz, Cruzinhas, Ilha; southbound via Faial and Porto da Cruz
b: northbound via Ribeiro Frio, Ilha; southbound via Cruzinhas and Ribeiro Frio
c: does not call at Ilha de São Jorge
d: calls at Ilha de São Jorge

110 Funchal · Boqueirão (via Caniço and Nogueira; journey time 40min)

Departs Funchal: 07.45•, 09.15+, 09.45+, 12.30*, 15.30+, 16.00□, 16.15+, 18.30#
Departs Boqueirão: 07.30*, 08.45#, 10.00+, 10.30+, 13.45*, 17.00+

111 Funchal · Achadinha (via Ribeirinha; journey time 1h)

Departs Funchal: 07.30+, 08.30+, 10.15+, 13.00, 15.45+, 18.15+, 19.05+, 19.45+
Departs Achadinha: 06.45+, 07.15+, 07.45+, 09.15+, 11.00+, 12.15+, 13.45, 16.30+

113 Funchal · Caniçal (via ⚓ and Machico; journey time 1h10min)

Departs Funchal: 07.30, 08.30*SL, 09.00SL, 11.15*SL, 12.15RS, 13.30•RS, 13.45+RS, 14.30*SL, 15.00+, 15.00•SL, 15.30*SL, 15.45•RS, 16.30•SL, 17.15*, 18.15+*SL, 19.00•SL, 19.30+, 19.45□, 20.00+RS, 21.00•RS, 22.30RS

Departs Caniçal: 05.45*, 06.45, 07.30*, 08.00+, 08.30+, 09.30, 10.20*SL, 11.40*SL, 11.55•*SL, 12.55+SL, 13.00□SL, 13.55*SL, 14.00§SL, 17.00SL, 18.00*SL, 19.00•SL, 19.40*SL, 21.00§

SLgoes on to/returns from São Lourenço Point; RSterminates at/returns from Ribeira Sêca. **See other symbol codes opposite.**

114 Funchal • Nogueira (via Caniço; journey time approximately 45min)
Departs Funchal: 06.30, 07.35, 08.45§, 09.30+, 10.00§, 11.15, 13.45*, 14.30, 16.30, 17.15+,
17.40, 18.25+, 18.50, 19.20*, 20.30, 22.00, 22.45+, 23.30, 00.15+
Departs Nogueira: 06.00, 07.00, 07.30+, 08.00+, 08.15, 09.25§, 10.15+, 10.40§, 11.55, 14.30*,
15.15, 17.15, 18.00+, 18.20, 19.30, 21.15, 22.15+, 22.45, 23.30+

115 Funchal • Estreito da Calheta • Paúl do Mar (journey time 2h50min)
Departs Funchal 16.05, 16.30+
Departs Paul do Mar 05.45 and Estreito 06.00

123 Funchal • Campanário (journey time 1h05min)
Departs Funchal: 11.30+, 13.00+, 18.00#; *Departs Campanário:* 12.40+, 14.30+

127 Ribeira Brava • Boa Morte (journey time 20min) • Fontes (journey time 30min)
Departs Ribeira Brava: 08.15+, 08.45§, 11.10, 13.10+   *Departs Fontes:* 08.45, 11.35
The buses at 08.45 and 11.10 go only to Boa Morte; return from Boa Morte at 09.10, 11.35.

132 Santana • Arco de São Jorge (journey time approximately 55min)
Departs Santana: 06.00+; *Departs Arco:* 18.00+

138 Funchal • Cabanas, São Jorge (routing varies; see a-d below)
Departs Funchal: 11.30+a/d, 16.30•a/c, 18.00+b/c, 19.10+a/c
Departs Cabanas: 05.10+b/c/d, 06.40+b (begins at Santana), 09.45•a/c, 10.00+a
a: northbound via Porto da Cruz and Faial; southbound via Faial and Porto da Cruz
b: northbound via Ribeiro Frio and Faial; southbound via Faial and Ribeiro Frio
c: calls at Cruzinhas; d) calls at Ilha de São Jorge
For times to intermediate destinations such as Ribeiro Frio compare bus 103.

139 Funchal • Porto Moniz and Santa (via Encumeada; journey time 3h30min; see also bus 80 for a 'round the island' trip)
Departs Funchal 09.00, 10.00+a, 17.35*
Departs Porto Moniz 05.15*+, 16.30+⥺ (from Porto Moniz, not Santa)
a: via Via Rápida to Ribeira Brava, then south coast and finally via Ponta do Pargo

142 Funchal • Ponta do Pargo (journey time 3h45min)
Departs Funchal: 08.05a, 12.00+⥺, 16.05•, 17.35+
Departs Ponta do Pargo: 05.30▫, 06.30•, 07.45+, 11.15+⥺, 13.45+ (via Paul do Mar), 14.35⥺
a: arrives Ribeira Brava 09.20, Formiga 10.00, Recta das Canhas 10.20, Prazeres 11.30, Ponta do Pargo 12.00;;
the bus departing Ponta do Pargo at 14.35 passes Prazeres at about 15.05. *All times are approximate!*

148 Funchal • Boa Morte (journey time 1h15min)
Departs Funchal: 13.05*, 18.05*; *Departs Boa Morte:* 06.50*, 14.30*

150 São Vicente • Santa (journey time 45min)
Departs São Vicente: 10.25, 16.30; *Departs Santa:* 14.00

154 Funchal • Cabo Girão (journey time 1h)
Departs Funchal: 08.50+, 10.35▫, 11.45+, 17.00*, 19.00+; *Departs Cabo Girão:* 11.50§, 12.50+,
18.00+

156 Funchal • Machico • Maroços • Porto da Cruz • (Faial)

Funchal	08.00*	10.30	11.45	11.45	13.15+	16.00*	16.30+
Machico	08.50*	11.20	12.25	12.25	14.05+	16.50*	17.15+
Maroços	09.05*	11.40a	12.35	12.50a	14.20+	17.05*	17.25+a
Pto da Cruz	00.00	11.50	00.00	13.00	00.00	00.00	17.50
Faial	00.00	00.00	00.00	00.00	00.00	00.00	18.00
Faial	06.45+	00.00	00.00	00.00	00.00	00.00	00.00
Pto da Cruz	07.00+	09.00+	11.50*	12.15•	13.00+	14.00+¶	15.00▫
Maroços	07.20+a	09.15+a	12.15*a	12.40•a	13.40+a	14.15+¶a	15.25▫a
Machico	07.30+	09.30+	12.45*	13.00	13.55+	14.30+¶	15.45▫
Funchal	08.05+	10.05+	13.10*	00.00	15.00+	00.00	16.45▫

Not all 156 buses are shown here; several others begin from/end at Machico
a: stops at Bar Fonte Vermelha near the Maroços Tunnel (best access to the Levada do Caniçal)

00.00 no service; +Mon-Fri; ■not on 31 Dec or 1 Jan; ▫only Saturdays; *not Sundays or holidays; ‡only Mon/ Wed/Fri; •only Sundays/holidays; ••only Sundays; †not Sundays or the first Saturday in Sept.; #not Saturdays; §Sat/Sun/holidays only; ¶in the school season only; ❖except 1, 6 Jan, 25, 26 Dec, via the coastal road and Ponta do Sol; **only on holidays; ▲Mondays to Saturdays, also holidays; ++Tue, Wed, Thur, Fri only; ⥺ via the Via Rapida and/or the Encumeada Tunnel

HORARIOS DO FUNCHAL (operators of the orange town buses)

A helpful plan for tourists, showing all town bus routes, fare zones and departure times of most interest to tourists is available from the Horarios office in Anadia Shopping (11 on the town plan) and information kiosks on the Avenida do Mar (see *i* symbol on the town plan on pages 10-11); ask for the 'Mini-Guide'. Timetables for all routes should be available free from the same office or the information kiosk just east of the Electricity Museum (no 33 on the plan). Weekly tourist passes are available *(you must show your passport)*. Or buy a 'double ticket' (*bilhete duplo;* also available in carnets of five tickets); these give you two bus journeys (not necessarily return trips) for little more than the cost of one. Otherwise, pay the driver as you board (keep small notes and coins handy).

It is not possible to list all departure times in the limited space below; where specific services *are* shown, only the departure times you are most likely to use are listed. Note also that these departure times change frequently; re-check departure times at the bus shelters shown on the town plan. **Or better still, download their map of routes and all the timetables you require in advance of your visit;** the Horarios web site (www.horariosdofunchal.pt) is super-efficient! Note on this web site that '2a a 6a feira' = Mon-Fri; Sábado = Sat; Domingo = Sun; S = departure; D = return.

1 Lombada ('Ponta da Laranjeira' bus; journey time approx. 30min) ∎

2 Quebradas ('Papagaio Verde' bus; journey time approx. 30min) ∎

3 Lombada (journey time approx 30min) ∎

4 Amparo (journey time approx. 20min)
Services too numerous to list; generally every 20 minutes (hourly on weekends).

6 Lido (journey time approx. 20min) ∎
Restricted Sunday service, except in summer. Check at the bus stop!

8 Madeira Shopping (journey time approx. 30min) ∎

11 Trapiche (journey time approx. 30min)
Services too numerous to list; generally half-hourly (hourly on weekends), but there is a two-hour gap in both directions between 14.00 and 16.00.
A 10A 'Chamorra' bus also serves Trapiche with equal frequency (including a service at around 15.00 on weekends), but be sure to ask the driver if the bus is going to Trapiche!

16 Madeira Shopping (journey time approx. 30min)* ∎

20, 21 Monte (journey time approx. 30min) ∎ **see also bus 22**
You can walk between Monte and Babosa in 10 minutes, past the Monte Palace Gardens and cable car station.

22 Babosas (journey time approx. 30min) ∎ **see also buses 20, 21**
You can walk between Monte and Babosas in 10 minutes, past the Monte Palace Gardens and cable car station.

29 Romeiros (via the Jardim Botânico; journey time approx. 30min)
Departs Funchal: 07.00*, 07.20*, 07.45, 08.20*, 08.50, 09.55•, 10.30*, 11.00, 12.05+, 12.35, 13.05, 13.30, 15.30, 17.35, 18.00+, 18.35, 19.00+, 19.35
Departs Romeiros: 08.15, 08.45*, 9.20, 10.35•, 11.05*, 11.40, 12.40+, 13.05, 13.35, 14.05, 16.05, 18.10, 18.35+, 19.10, 19.25+. 20.10, 21.10

30 Jardim Botânico ('Largo do Miranda' bus; journey time approx. 15min)
Hourly or every two hours every day of the week.

31 Jardim Botânico (journey time approx. 15min) ∎

36 Palheiro Ferreiro ('Lombo da Quinta' bus; journey time approx. 25min) ∎
This bus terminates 300m/yds below the southern entrance to the Palheiro Gardens.

37 Palheiro Ferreiro (journey time approx. 25min)
Departs Funchal: 07.35, 08.50+, 12.00, 13.10, 16.45, 17.30+, 18.10, 19.20
Departs Palheiro Ferreiro: 12.35, 13.50, 17.40, 18.05+, 18.50, 19.20+, 19.50
Stops at the entrance to the Palheiro Gardens; also at the Levada dos Tornos on the ER102.

45 Funchal • Levada dos Piornais ('Nazaré' bus; journey time approx 10min) ∎

47 São João Latrão (journey time approx. 20min)
Departs Funchal: 08.00, 08.50+, 11.00, 12.40, 13.10+, 13.40, 16.05*, 17.20+
Departs São João Latrão (ER201): 11.40, 13.15, 13.40+, 14.10, 16.50*, 18.30

91 Barrreira • Trapiche (shuttle bus; change at Trapiche for Bus 11 or 10A)
Departs Barreira (for Trapiche): 09.45, 12.00, 13.00, 14.00, 14.35, 17.38, 18.11
Departs Trapiche (for Barreira): 09.34, 11.50, 12.39, 13.39, 14.29, 17.32, 18.05

∎Services too numerous to list and growing all the time; please consult the Horarios web site; *not Sundays or holidays; #not Saturdays; +Mon-Fri; §Sat/Sun/holidays only; •Sundays only

● *Index*

Geographical entries only are included here; for other entries, see Contents, page 3. A page number in **bold type** indicates a photograph; a page number in *italics* a map (*TM* refers to the large-scale walking map on the reverse of the touring map). For pronunciation hints, see page 144. For buses, see Timetables index, page 138.

Pronunciation/translation of some index entries